An Antidote against Arminianism

Great Christian Books
Lindenhurst, New York

An Antidote against Arminianism

Christopher Ness

CHRISTOPHER NESS

AN
ANTIDOTE
AGAINST
ARMINIANISM:
OR
A TREATISE
TO ENERVATE AND CONFUTE ALL THE FIVE POINTS THEREOF:

VIZ.

PREDESTINATION GROUNDED UPON MAN'S FORESEEN WORKS—UNIVERSAL REDEMPTION—SUFFICIENT GRACE IN ALL—THE POWER OF MAN'S FREE-WILL IN CONVERSION—AND, THE POSSIBILITY OF TRUE SAINTS FALLING AWAY TOTALLY AND FINALLY.

RECOMMENDED BY DR. OWEN, AND PUBLISHED FOR PUBLIC GOOD.

BY CHRISTOPHER NESS.

London: Printed in the Year 1700.

FOURTH EDITION,

BEING THE THIRD AS REVISED AND CORRECTED, WITH MANY ADDITIONS, NOTES, ETC.,

BY J. A. JONES,

Minister of the Gospel, Mitchell-street, St Luke's.

LONDON:
PUBLISHED BY J. BENNETT, 4, THREE-TUN-PASSAGE, IVY LANE, PATERNOSTER-ROW.

1836.

Great Christian Books
is an imprint of Rotolo Media
160 37th Street Lindenhurst, New York 11757
(631) 956-0998

©2012 Rotolo Media / Great Christian Books
All rights reserved under International and Pan-American Copyright Conventions. No part of this book maybe reproduced in any form, or by any means, electronic or mechanical, including photocopying, and informational storage and retrieval systems without the expressed written permission from the publisher, except in the case of brief quotations embodied in articles or reviews or promotional/advertising/catalog materials. For additional information or permissions, address all inquiries to the publisher.

> Ness, Christopher, 1621–1705
> An Antidote to Arminianism / by Christopher Ness
>   p.   cm.
> A "A Great Christian Book" book
> GREAT CHRISTIAN BOOKS an imprint of Rotolo Media
> ISBN 978-1-61010-480-7
> Recommended Dewey Decimal Classification: 234
> Suggested Subject Headings:
> 1. Religion—Christian literature—Soteriology
> 2. Christianity—The Bible—Calvinism
> I. Title

Book and cover design are by www.michaelrotolo.com. This book is typeset in the Minion typeface by Adobe Inc. and is quality-manufactured on acid-free paper stock. To discuss the publication of your Christian manuscript or out-of-print book, please contact us.

Manufactured in the United States of America

CONTENTS

EDITOR'S PREFACE	9
AUTHOR'S PREFACE	17
OF ARMINIANISM IN GENERAL	21
1. OF PREDESTINATION	25
2. OF UNIVERSAL REDEMPTION	67
3. OF FREE-WILL IN THE FALLEN STATE, AND OF EFFECTUAL VOCATION OR CONVERSION TO GOD	83
4. OF FINAL PERSEVERANCE	97
CONCLUSION	117

EDITOR'S PREFACE
by J.A. JONES Editor of
the FOURTH EDITION (OF 1836)

Christian Reader,

I present to you a new edition of a book, diminutive in size, yet large and exceeding ponderous in relation to the glorious foundation-truths and doctrines of the gospel, which are here throughout handled so scripturally, and withal so luminous, that (as hath been expressed by some very competent judges) "there is no work of the kind that can excel it."

Arminianism, that foul heresy, which may be said to be the root and core of all heretical false doctrine, is here completely stripped of its deceitful covering; and (as it were) anatomically dissected, laid open, and made bare. Free-will, the great idol of fallen man, is thrown down from its assumed eminence, and cast to the moles and the bats; and free-grace, yea, the God of all grace, is exalted, and viewed as seated on the throne of His Glory.

I would honestly tell the reader, at the very onset, that he will not approve of the contents of this work, provided he is, in the least, dependent on any performances of his own, to recommend him to the notice and approbation of the great I AM. The characters who eat their own bread, and who wear their own apparel (Isa. iv. 1), will here find no food that they can relish, and no raiment suited to clothe their self-righteous persons. There is nothing in these pages but what must ever prove obnoxious to the pride of the human heart, as unhumbled by divine grace. The sovereignty of Jehovah; the free-love of God, as displayed in the choice of the Church in Christ Jesus before time;

divine Predestination in its various properties, here so masterly proved; Redemption as limited by price, and the redeemed ones discovered by invincible power; the glorious certainty of true saints persevering to the end for—

> *"The feeblest saint shall win the day,*
> *Though death and hell obstruct the way;"*

Or, as in a word—salvation all of grace, from first to last, from election to glorification;—the creature nothing; the triune God, all in all;—yes, reader, by long experience, do I know, that an unflinching statement of these glorious truths cannot fail to draw forth the latent rancor of the unregenerate mind.

But let the case be fairly stated; and, in the strong and energetic language of the great Toplady, let me inquire—

> "And what indeed is Predestination, but God's determinate plan of action? And what is providence but the evolution of that plan? In his decree, God resolved within himself, what he would do, and what he would permit to be done: by his providence, this effective and permissive will, passes into external act, and has its positive accomplishment. So that the purpose of God, as it were, draws the outlines, and providence lays on the colors. What that designed, this completes; what that ordained, this executes. Predestination is analogous to the mind and intention; providence, to the hand and agency, of the artificer. The Lord is incapable of mistake, he knows no levity of will. He cannot be surprised with any unforeseen inconveniences. His throne is in heaven, and his kingdom ruleth over all. God's sovereign will is the first link, his unalterable decree is the second, and his all-active providence the third, in the great chain of causes. What his will determined, that his decree established, and his providence (either mediately or immediately) effects. His will was the adorable spring of all; his decree marked out the channel; and his providence directs the stream. Of this I am assured, that echo does not reverberate sound so punctually, as the actual disposal

of things answers to God's predetermination concerning them. This cannot be denied without dethroning providence, and setting up fortune in its room. There is no alternative. I defy all the sophistry of man, to strike out a middle way. He that made all things, either directs all things he has made, or has consigned them over to chance. But, what is chance? A name for nothing. Arminianism, therefore, is atheism."

I would avail myself of the opportunity afforded me, in these my prefatory remarks, to say a few words to those Ministers of the Gospel who are continued faithful, and who are desirous of abiding faithful, even to the end.—Remember my brethren, that Israel's valiant ones are expected (especially in such a day as this) to be found surrounding the bed of Solomon, (which is the Church;) all of them holding swords, being expert in war; every man having his sword upon his thigh, because of fear in the night. I pray you consider it as your highest honor to stand fast without wavering. "O Timothy (says Paul) keep that which is committed to thy trust," 1 Tim. vi. 20, that good thing, (that blessed depositum) which was committed unto thee, keep by the Holy Ghost which dwelleth in us, 2 Tim. i. 14. Aim to have a full apprehension and knowledge of the Truth, and that upon its own proper grounds, and principles; and part not with one grain of God's precious Truth, no not for the dearest friend upon earth. Have nothing to do with the wrists of men, be careless of the pulse of their inclinations; fear not their frowns, court not their smiles. "Do I seek to please men? (saith the apostle) if I yet pleased men, I should not be the servant of Christ," Gal. i. 10. Every thing that is contrary to, and against the word of God, you must oppose. And Arminianism or free-will, is contrary thereto. Be not engaged then, in merely lopping off a few of the upper branches, but, let the axe be laid to the root of the tree; for remember that—Arminianism and Pelagianism (which is all one) is the very life and soul of Popery.

Holy Dr. Owen, in a *Charge at the Ordination of a Minister*, in 1682, only eleven months before his death; says,—

"I fear there is much loss of Truth, (not for want of light, nor yet for want of ability, but,) for want of love. I knew the contest we had for the Truths of the Gospel, before our national troubles began; and was an early person engaged in them. I knew those godly ministers, that did contend for truth, as for their lives and souls: and that all the opposition that was made against them, was never able to discourage them. Divine Truths are declining in our pulpits, not for want of skill, but for want of love. We scarce hear one word of them now. We are almost ashamed to mention them in the Church. And he that doth preach them, will be sure to expose himself to public derision and scorn. But we must not be ashamed of Truth. Formerly we could not meet with a godly minister, but the error of Arminianism was looked upon by him, as the ruin and poison of the souls of men. Such godly men did tremble at it, wrote, and disputed against it: but now it is not so. Now, though we tacitly own the doctrines of the gospel, the love of them seems greatly decayed, and the power thereof almost lost. But we have got no ground by it; we are not more holy, more fruitful, than we were when we preached those Truths, and attended diligently unto them. They were the life of the reformation; and they were the soul and life of those, who are gone home before us: they found the power and comfort of them in life, and in death also; and they now find the Truth of them in Glory! Let us then, for the remainder of our days, buy the Truth, and sell it not*."

---

* "The eternal Predestination of Almighty God, that fountain of all spiritual blessings, of all the effects of God's love derived to us through Christ; the demolishing of this Rock of our salvation, hath been the chief endeavour of all the patrons of human self-sufficiency. And this is their FIRST attempt to attain their Second proposed end, namely, that of building a Tower (a Babel, Gen. xi. 4), from the top whereof they may mount into heaven; whose Foundation is nothing but the Sand of their own Free-will and Endeavours. Our Arminians have invented a multitude of new notions, and terms, to Obscure the doctrine:— "Election, they say, is either

Some persons would fain persuade us, that, the Arminian controversy hath very much changed its aspect, since the days of Christopher Ness; and, that when it is now agitated (which they desire for charity sake may be as seldom as possible) it turns upon other points, than those contained in this book. No, no; the subtle enemy may dexterously maneuver to fight behind a masked battery; or, to change, in words merely, his polemical ground; but the dark aspect of Arminianism is not changed. And it may be said thereof, as of Amalek, "Because the hand of Amalek is against the Throne of the Lord, therefore, the Lord hath sworn, that the Lord will have war with Amalek, from generation to generation," Exod. xvii. 16.

Modern Arminianism, is but ancient Pelagianism, which reared up in the second century; and Pelagianism is Popery; and Popery is (yea all is) but as another name for man's free-will, in opposition to God's free-grace. 'Tis All One.

We do indeed live in a day of sad declensions from the Truth. Dr. Gill, in his sermon, entitled, *Watchman, What of the Night?* preached by him, Dec. 27, 1750, more than 85 years ago, writes as in a prophetic spirit—

> "A night is coming on; the shadows of the evening are stretching out apace upon us, and the signs of the even-tide are very manifest, and which will shortly appear yet more and more. Coldness and indifference in spiritual things; a want of affection to God, Christ, his people, truths, and ordinances, may easily be observed. The first love is left; iniquity abounds; and the love of

---

legal or evangelical, general or particular, complete or incomplete, revocable or irrevocable, peremptory or not peremptory;" with I know not how many more Distinctions of ONE SINGLE ETERNAL ACT of Almighty God: whereof there is neither sign, nor token, in the whole Bible.

Reason, Scripture, God himself, ALL must give place to any absurdities, if they stand in the Arminian's way; bringing in their IDOL with shouts, and preparing his THRONE by claiming the cause of their predestination to be in themselves."

—Owen's Display of Arminianism

many waxes cold, and it will wax yet colder and colder; issuing in a neglect of the ministers of the gospel, when professors will be shy of them, and carefully shun them, will not care to own them, or to speak to them, and much less receive them into their houses; and still less hear them preach. As yet, it is not totally dark, or quite night; it is a sort of twilight with us, between clear and dark, between day and night."

It has been getting darker and darker, from the hour that sermon was preached. The Lord knoweth what is before us. But, my dear brethren in the work of the Christian ministry—

"...let none of these things move you from your close adherence to the truth; strive together for the faith of it, against the common enemy. Abide by it, though the greater number of professors are against it; and those, the rich, the wise, the learned; and though it may be attended with reproach and persecution. Be of good courage, take heart, consider you are engaged in a good cause, and are fighting under the command of the great Captain of your salvation: you are sure of victory in the end, and the issue will be, a crown of life. Keep close to the Word of God; try the doctrines, try the spirits thereby, whether they be of God. The Word of the Lord is a lamp to you, and a light for you; you will do well to make good use of it. When is light so useful as in the night-season? It is so now; therefore take your lamp, or light, in your hand, and walk closely by the Word of God, whereunto ye do well to take heed, as unto a light that shineth in a dark place. Blessed is that servant, whom his Lord when he cometh, shall find so doing." —John Gill

Reader! try the contents of this book, by the Lord's unerring standard—the Bible. Scripture-proofs are plentifully set before you, in every page: examine well for yourself; prove all things, and hold fast that which is good.

In my former editions I informed the reader, and I now repeat the information;—that, I have taken the liberty both to retrench, and also much enlarge in this volume, from the original, by Ness.

In a doctrinal point of view there is no alteration; in mutual agreement in the truth, we have walked together throughout. The phraseology and mode of expression used by Ness, in 1700, needed revision, to render the work acceptable to readers in the year 1836. Also, Latin, Greek, and Hebrew words, and phrases, occurring in almost every page of the original, the book in its primitive dress was by no means suitable, nay, it could not be perused with profit, so as to be fully understood, by average readers. My former editions have been appreciated by many of the children of God; and the Lord's glory, and his people's profit, has been before me in this edition also. O may a divine blessing accompany it, to the establishment of many souls in the truth, and to the reclaiming of others from the many paths of error.

Reader, farewell!
I am, yours in the Lord,
JOHN ANDREWS JONES

42 Moneyers Street
Hoxton, London   March 24, 1836.

AUTHOR'S PREFACE

Candid Reader,

Observe these few considerations: although this small manual be very little in itself and substance, yet ought it not therefore to be despised; for,

First,—We read how the mighty angel of the Covenant had a very little book open in his hand, Rev. x. 2; yet this little book contained the great concerns of the Redeemer's little, little flock; a double diminutive as Christ calls them in Luke, xii. 32. And that little book was not shut nor sealed, but it was open. 'Tis the work of Antichrist to keep it shut. Yea, it must also be eaten, take it and eat it up, Rev. x. 10; that is, it must go down and be hid in our hearts (thy word have I hid in mine heart, Psalm cxix. 11); then the simplest soul may have right conceptions of it, The word [is then] very nigh unto thee, in thy mouth, and in thy heart, that thou mayest do it, Deut. xxx. 14.

Secondly,—This little book hath cost me great study and labour to compose it, that it might contain the very cream and quintessence of the best Authors on this subject. Moreover, it hath cost me likewise many ardent prayers to God, and many earnest wrestlings with God, that I might not be one of those that rebel against the light, Job, xxiv. 13; but that in His light I might see light, Psalm xxxvi. 9; and to have mine eyes anointed with Christ's eye-salve, Rev. iii. 18, that I might see clearly into these profound points, which hath so very much puzzled the

Christian world. As blessed Athanasius sighed out in his day, "The world is overrun with Arianism;" so 'tis the sad sigh of our present times, the christian world is overrun, yea, overwhelmed with the flood of Arminianism: which cometh, as it were, out of the mouth of the Serpent, that he might cause the woman [the Church] to be carried away of the flood thereof, Rev. xii. 15.

Thirdly,—Lest this overflowing deluge of Arminianism should bring destruction upon us, there is great need that some servants of Christ should run to stop the further spreading of this plague and leprosy. Thus Moses stood in the gap, and prevented the destruction of Israel, Psalm cvi. 23. Also Num. xvi. 48. He stood between the dead and the living, and the plague was stayed. And the neglect of this duty the Lord complains of, that he found none of his servants to stand in the gap, etc. O Israel thy Prophets are like the foxes in the deserts. Ye have not gone up into the gaps, neither made up the hedge for the house of Israel to stand in the battle in the day of the Lord. With lies ye have made the heart of the righteous sad, whom I have not made sad; and strengthened the hands of the wicked, by promising him life, Ezek. xiii. 5, 22. While I was considering these things, the Lord stirred up my spirit, to do as is done in common conflagrations, when every one runs with the best bucket he can get, wherewith to quench the devouring flames, and to stop them, that they may not lay waste all before them.

Fourthly,—When I had completed this short Compendium, I shewed it to Dr. John Owen, Mr. Nicholas Lockier, and Mr. George Griffith; who all unanimously approved of it, and wrote an epistle commendatory to it, subscribing it with all their three hands, which is too large here to insert, but the truth of the premises I do hereby affirm.

Lastly,—As a little map doth represent a large country at one view, which will take much time to travel over; so this book is multum in parvo, much in a little. Read it seriously without partiality, and the Lord give you understanding in all things.

So prayeth—

Yours in the best Bonds,

Christopher Ness

Sept. 30, 1700

OF ARMINIANISM IN GENERAL

It hath ever been the lot of truth (like the Lord of it) to be crucified between thieves on the right hand and thieves on the left. Truth's enemies, on all hands, are various. While some men consider the Bible to be an imposition on the world, and treat salvation by Christ as mere priestcraft and deception, there are others who tell us they have Christ, and are one with Christ, and yet with audacious effrontery cry down the ordinances of the gospel, and consider the means of grace as too burdensome for a free-born conscience, and too low and carnal for a seraphic spirit. There is as much beyond the truth as on this side of it; as much in outrunning the flock of Christ and the Lamb that leads them, as in straggling and loitering behind. Truth hath evermore observed the golden mean.

The Socinians decry the divinity of Christ and His satisfaction, as if His sufferings were exemplary only, not expiatory. The Roman Catholics turn the true worship of God into will worship, and teach their own traditions for the commandments of God, spoiling God's institutions with man's inventions. And the Arminians do call the justice of God to the bar of reason; they dare confidently wade in the deep ocean of divine mysteries, and in stating the decrees of God, where blessed Paul could find no bottom, but cried out "O the depth" etc. (Rom 11:33); they dare undertake to fetch the Apostle from off his nonplus, saying, "God *foresaw* that Jacob would believe, and that Esau would not believe; therefore, the one was loved and the other hated." Thus Arminius' school teacheth deeper divinity than what Paul learned in the third heaven. And they do not only with the Socinians gratify the pride of man's reason, but also the pride of man's will, in extenuating and lessening both the guilt and filth of original sin; even as Popery, their elder sister, doth gratify the pride of outward sense.

Hence Dr. Leighton calls Arminianism:

> "the Pope's Benjamin, the last and greatest monster of the man of sin; the elixir of Anti-Christianism; the mystery of the mystery of iniquity; the Pope's cabinet; the very quintessence of equivocation."

Alike hereunto Mr. Rous (Master of Eton College) addeth, saying,

> "Arminianism is the spawn of Popery, which the warmth of favour may easily turn into frogs of the bottomless pit." And what are the new Arminians but the varnished offspring of the old Pelagians, that makes the grace of God to lackey it at the foot, or rather, the will of man? that makes the sheep to keep the shepherd? that puts God into the same extremity with Darius, who would gladly have saved Daniel but could not (Da 6:14)?

What else can their doctrine signify which they call a prescience or foreknowledge in God, the truth of which depends, not on the decree of God, but on the free-will of the creature? This is to make the creature have no dependence on the Creator, and to fetter Divine Providence. Thus that fatal necessity, which they would lay at our doors, unavoidably remains at theirs, and (according to their scheme) God must say thus to man, "O My poor creature? that fatal fortune which hath harmed you must be endured more than bewailed, for it was from all eternity, before My providence. I could not hinder, I could not but consent to those fatal contingencies; and unavoidable Fate hath, whether I will or not, pronounced the inevitable sentence." What else is this but to overthrow all those graces of Faith, Hope, etc., to expectorate (to cast off) all vital godliness; and to pull the great Jehovah Himself out of His throne of glory, setting up dame Fortune to be worshipped in His stead?

These and many other great abominations have been discovered in the "chambers of imagery" in our days, and are nothing but measuring supernatural mysteries with the crooked measuring rod of degenerate reason. "Wisdom is too high for a fool" (Prv 24:7). In these points it was once well said, "Give me a mortified reason," for, to prescribe to God's infinite understanding, and to allow Him no reasons to guide His determinations by, but what we are acquainted with, is extremely arrogant. Reason must neither be the rule to measure faith by, nor the judge of it. We may give a reason of our believing, to wit, "because it is written," but not of all things believed, as why Jacob was loved and Esau hated before they had done either good or evil—*this was the counsel of God's own will*. Touching such sublime mysteries our faith stands upon two sure bottoms: the first is,—that the wisdom, and the power of God doth infinitely transcend ours; so it may reveal matters far above our reach; the second is; that whatsoever God reveals is undoubtedly true, and to be believed, although the bottom of it cannot be fathomed by the sounding line of our reason; because man's reason is not absolute, but variously limited, perplexed with his own frailty, and defective in its own acting.

Chapter One

OF PREDESTINATION

That the reader may have clear views of the doctrine of Predestination, I shall, first, state that doctrine as revealed in the Bible; second, consider the Arminian's view of it, namely, that Predestination is conditional upon the foresight of faith, works, perseverance, etc., and, thirdly, answer the objections brought by the Arminians against the Scriptural doctrine of Election and Predestination.

The Doctrine of Predestination

Predestination is the decree of God, by which (according to the counsel of His own will) He fore-ordained some of mankind to eternal life, and refused or passed by others; for the praise of His glorious mercy and justice. Some are vessels of mercy, others are vessels of wrath. *"Hath not the potter power over the clay, of the same lump to make one vessel unto honour, and another unto dishonour? What if God, willing to show His wrath, and to make His power known, endured with much long-suffering the vessels of wrath fitted to destruction; And that he might make known the riches of His glory on the vessels of mercy, which He had afore prepared unto glory"* (Romans 9:21-23)

In a great house are various vessels both for use and ornament; vessels of honour, and vessels of dishonour, (2 Tm 2:20); and the master of the house hath a right to, and can wisely use, all his vessels, even as he shall think proper. God hath His use even of Pharaoh and of the church's greatest enemies; if it be but scullion work, to brighten vessels of mercy by them. God hath appointed the Elect unto Glory; and He hath by the eternal and most free purpose of His will fore-ordained all the means thereunto; such as redemption by Christ, regeneration by the Holy Ghost, effectual calling and conversion, justification in the court of conscience by saving faith in Jesus' merits, sanctification in the heart by the Spirit, producing holy living and holy walking with God and man. And these blessed participators are "kept by the power of God through faith unto salvation" (1Pe 1:5). "Whom He did predestinate, them He also called: and whom He called, them he also justified: and whom He justified, them He also glorified. What shall we then say to these things?" (Rom 8:30, 31). We will say with the apostle, "God hath not appointed us to wrath, but to obtain salvation" (1Th 5:9).

It is called destination, as it comprehends a determined order of the means to the end; and predestination, because God appointed this order in and with Himself before the actual existence of those things so ordered. The Greek word signifies a fore-separated for God's special use; as Israel was separated from among all the nations of the world to be God's peculiar inheritance. "I am the Lord your God, which have separated you from other people" (Lv 20:24). "The Lord thy God hath chosen thee to be a special people unto Himself, above all people that are upon the face of the earth" (Dt 7:6). I have separated you to become vessels of mercy, members of Christ, and temples of the

Holy Ghost, before all time, even from all eternity. As Divine prescience is sometimes largely taken for predestination, "God hath not cast away His people which He foreknew" (Rom 11:2), that is, whom He did predestinate; so, in like manner, predestination is taken strictly and in part for election itself (Rom 8:30; Eph 1:5). I shall handle it accordingly in this following treatise, using the words Election and Predestination promiscuously.

Predestination is also called a Divine decree, for in it is the determinate counsel of God, and the counsel of His own will, in bringing to pass such ends by such and such means. "For of a truth against thy holy child Jesus, whom thou hast anointed, both Herod, and Pontius Pilate, with the Gentiles, and the people of Israel, were gathered together, For to do whatsoever thy hand and thy counsel determined before to be done" (Acts 4:27, 28). "Having predestinated us... according to the good pleasure of His will" (Eph 1:5). "Being predestinated according to the purpose of Him who worketh all things after the counsel of His own will" (Eph 1:11). The election and predestination of the Lord is, in Scriptural language, termed the "hand," the "determinate counsel," the "purpose," the "good pleasure" of God (Acts 2:23; Eph 1:9).

The Divine decree of Predestination hath various properties; it is eternal, unchangeable, absolute, free, discriminating, and extensive.

The First Property of the Divine Decree;
It is ETERNAL

This is proved from the following reasons; —

1. God's internal and immanent acts are the same with His essence: such an act is the Divine decree: and, therefore, as God's essence is eternal, so His decree must be eternal also. Now the decree is God's decreeing, because whatever is in God is God; it is God Himself by one eternal act, decreeing and determining

whatsoever should come to pass unto the praise of His own glory.

2. The second reason is deduced from the simplicity of God, which is, God considered as one mere and perfect act, without any composition or succession. There can be no more a new thought, a new intent, or a new purpose in God, than there can be a new God. Whatever God thinks He ever thought, and always doth and will think. Whatever God purposes He always purposed, and ever and doth and will purpose. He saith, "I know the thoughts I think toward you, saith the Lord, thoughts of peace, and not of evil, to give you an expected end" (Jer 29:11). As He cannot know anything new, neither can He intend anything new, for His name is, I AM. He takes not new counsels, as man, neither draws up new determinations.

3. The third reason is taken from Christ. If Christ was the Lamb slain from the foundation of the world (as He is called, Re 13:8), then predestination to life must needs be before time, because Christ is the Foundation of election. We are elected in Him. "According as He hath chosen us in Him before the foundation of the world" (Eph 1:4); and predestinated by Him, "Having predestinated us unto the adoption of children by Jesus Christ to Himself" (Eph 1:5). Christ is the means. Now the end cannot be of a later date and determination than the means to that end; they have relations to each other. And if Christ be the eternal purpose of the Father, the act of electing in Christ must needs be His eternal purpose also.

4. Scripture expressly proves the eternity of the decree, saying, it was "before the world began" (2 Tm 1:9; Titus 1:2); and "before the foundation of the world" (Eph 1:4); and it was an "eternal purpose which He purposed in Christ Jesus our Lord" (Eph 3:11).

5. It is the royal prerogative of the great Jehovah to order as well as appoint things that are coming and that shall come: "I

appointed the ancient people, and the things that are coming and shall come" (Isa 44:7). None can appoint God the time. He saith, "Who is like Me? and who will appoint Me the time?" (Jer 50:44). Hence time is said to travail with those eternal decrees of God, and brings forth the accomplishment of them in their proper season; and the decree will bring forth ("Before the decree bring forth," Zep 2:2). Every thing hath its accomplishment in time, which was decreed to fall out from all eternity.

6. If human concerns have this encomium that "these are ancient things" (1Ch 4:22), how much more the Divine decree, which is not the work of yesterday! If the negative part of predestination (the ungodly) were "of old ordained" (Jude 4), then much more the positive, God's purpose of loving Jacob, as well as hating Esau, was before they had done "either good or evil" (Rom 9:11).

Objection

Some may object, saying, We grant God's prescience or foreknowledge to be eternal, but not His predestination; that choice or election mentioned in 1 Cor 1:27-29 must be a temporal, not an eternal, election.

Answers

1. With God, the knowledge of things that shall come to pass must follow the decree of it; for things must first be decreed, and then foreseen in that being which they have in the decree; in this sense prescience presupposes predestination. "Known unto God are all His works from the beginning of the world" (Acts 15:18). God hath not an imperfect but a thorough foreknowledge of all future things; the means and the end; not only as they may be, but also as they shall be, by His Divine determination.

2. Prescience, or fore-knowledge, is taken for God's love from eternity. "Whom He did foreknow He also did predestinate" (Rom 8:29); that is, "whom He fore-loved" so Zanchius reads it.

Whom He foreknew, not only with the knowledge of observation, but with the knowledge of approbation also; He foreknew them to be His. So it is predestination itself; and to grant an eternal prescience without an eternal predestination, is to break the links of that golden chain in Rom 8:29,30. "God hath not," and God will not, "cast away His people which He foreknew" (Rom 11:2).

3. Some grant a predestination eternal to the elect only, but to the non-elect only a prescience or naked foresight (without any pre-ordination), lest they should make God the author of the creature's sin and ruin. But these men fear where no fear is; for the worst evil that ever was committed in the world, to wit, the crucifying of the Prince of glory, Jesus Christ, did not only fall under the foreknowledge of God, but also under His determinate counsel, "Him being delivered by the determinate counsel and foreknowledge of God, ye have taken, and by wicked hands have crucified and slain" (Acts 2:23; 4:28); the taking and apprehension of Christ was not barely foreknown but unchangeably determined.

4. Even suppose it be granted that the apostle speaks of a temporal election, or choice, in 1 Cor 1:27, etc., yet that signifies no more than our vocation or calling; and temporal reprobation intimates no more than man's hard-heartedness. The accomplishment of both these is granted to be in time, so may not be confounded with this eternal decree of God; these are but fruits and effects of that eternal decree.

Inferences drawn from the foregoing:

1. Is God's love eternal? Then Satan cannot get beyond or between this love of God and us; for it was before the world was, and so before Satan was.

2. Augustine told a curious fool that asked what God did before the world was made, "that He made hell for such as him;" but this teaches us that God was choosing us to Himself before the world began. O wonderful!

3. If so, believer, then thy saintship and sufferings have eternal glory wrapped up in them. All this comfort is lost in the contrary doctrine.

The Second Property of the Divine Decree of Predestination;
It is UNCHANGEABLE

Hence it is compared to "mountains of brass" (Zec 6:1), and it is called, "immutability of his counsel" (Heb 6:17). This is made evident by sundry reasons, as:

1. The Divine decree hath an unchangeable fountain, to wit, the unchangeableness of God. "He is in one mind, and who can turn Him?" (Job 23:13). He desires and He doth it; no created being can interpose between the desire and the doing, to hinder their meeting together. "God is not a man, that He should lie; neither the son of man that He should repent" (Nu 23:19). "I am the Lord, I change not" (Mal 3:6); with Him is no "variableness, neither shadow of turning" (Jas 1:17). "The counsel of the Lord standeth for ever, the thoughts of his heart to all generations" (Ps 33:11). "There are many devices in a man's heart; nevertheless the counsel of the Lord, that shall stand" (Prv 19:21). Man is a poor changeable creature and changes his mind oftener than his garment, both from the darkness of his understanding and the perverseness of his will. He frequently sees something that he saw not before. But there is no such imperfection in God, all things are naked before Him, dissected, or with their faces upward. "Neither is there any creature that is not manifest in His sight; but all things are naked and opened unto the eyes of Him with whom we have to do" (Heb 4:13). He knows all His works (their natures and circumstances) as perfectly in the beginning of the world as He will do at the end of it. And He abides still in one mind when His dispensations are changed, for He decreed the change of them from all eternity.

2. The decree of Election stands upon an unchangeable foundation, that is to say, that Rock of ages, "Jesus Christ, the same yesterday, and today, and forever" (Heb 13:8). As the first Adam was the foundation stone in the decree of creation, so the last Adam, even Jesus, is the foundation stone in the decree of election. God hath blessed us in Him, yea, and we shall be blessed. He hath chosen us in Him; pardoned us in Him; sealed us in Him; built us up and completed us in Him; "According to His own purpose and grace, which was given us in Christ Jesus before the world began" (2 Tm 1:9). All those acts of grace are said to be in Christ, who hath blest us in Christ (Eph 1:3); chosen us in Him (Eph 1:4); pardoned us; "in whom we have redemption through His blood, the forgiveness of sins" (Eph 1:7); "in whom also after that ye believed, ye were sealed" (Eph 1:13); "rooted and built up in Him" (Col 2:7): and ye are "complete in Him" (Col 2:10).

Indeed, Christ Himself was under Divine ordination; He "verily was fore-ordained before the foundation of the world" (1Pe 1:20), and is called the elect stone (1Pe 2:6). Christ is the first person elected. "Behold My servant whom I uphold, Mine elect" (Isa 42:1; Mt 12:18). Christ was chosen as the Head, and we as His members; therefore are we said to be given to Christ. "Thine they were, and Thou gavest them Me" (Jn 17:6). Now, so long as this foundation standeth sure, so long doth the superstructure remain unchangeable. The temple stood firmly upon those two pillars, Jachin and Boza, i.e., stability and strength; so the decree of election standeth sure upon Christ the Foundation; and none can pluck an elect soul from off this Foundation. None can pluck any of Christ's out of His hands. Christ will lose none that are given to him; He will fulfil His Father's will by taking care of them all. "And this is the Father's will which hath sent Me, that of all which He hath given Me I should lose nothing, but should raise it up again at the last day" (Jn 6:39). "They shall never perish" (Jn 10:28).

3. 'Tis unchangeable, because it is a decree written in Heaven, and so above the reach of either angry men or enraged devils to cancel. "The Lord knoweth them that are His" (2 Tm 2:19), they are "the general assembly and church of the first-born, which are written in Heaven" (Heb 12:23). Thence it is called "the Lamb's book of life," which contains a catalog of the elect, determined by the unalterable counsel of God; which number can neither be increased nor diminished. This is to be rejoiced in above dominion over devils; "rather rejoice, because your names are in Heaven" (Lk 10:20); which, if our names may be written in Heaven today and blotted out tomorrow would be no such ground of joy. If the decrees of the Medes and Persians, which were but earthly writings, were unalterable (Da 6:8), how much more the decrees of the great God, written in Heaven, must be unchangeable. Must Pilate say, "What I have written I have written" (Jn 19:22); that is to say, "my writing shall not be altered," and shall not God say so much more? "I know (saith Solomon) that, whatsoever God doeth, it shall be for ever; nothing can be put to it, nor anything taken from it" (Eccl 3:14). "My counsel shall stand, and I will do all My pleasure... I have spoken it, I will also bring it to pass; I have purposed it, I will also do it" (Isa 46:10,11). The sun may sooner be stopped in his course than God hindered of His work or in His will. Nature, angels, devils, men, may all be resisted, and so miss of their design; not so God: for "who hath resisted His will?" All those chariots of human occurrences and dispensations come forth from between those mountains of brass, the unalterable decrees of God (Zec 6:1); and should it be granted that one soul may be blotted out of this book of life (this writing in Heaven) then it is possible that all may be so; and, by consequence, it may be supposed that that book may become empty, and useless as waste paper; and that Christ may be a head without a body.

4. 'Tis unchangeable, for the decree concerning the end includes the means to that end, and binds them altogether with

an unbreakable chain, it can never be refuted. The predestinated, called, justified, glorified ones, are the same (Rom 8:30). Therefore the purpose of God according to election must stand (Rom 9:11). God doth not decree the end without the means, nor the means without the end, but both together. As a purpose for building includes the hewing of stone, and squaring of timber, and all other materials for construction; and as a decree for war implies arms, horses, ammunition, and all warlike provisions; so here, all that are elected to salvation, are elected to sanctification also. God ordains to the means as well as to the end. "As many as were ordained to eternal life believed" (Acts 13:48). God hath ordained that we should walk in good works (Eph 2:10). We are elected unto obedience, through the "sanctification of the Spirit" (1Pe 1:2); therefore God hath promised to sanctify those whom He purposed to save. We teach with Augustine that, "Election is an ordaining to grace as well as to glory." In predestination, therefore, the means of salvation are no less absolutely decreed than salvation itself. We may not conceive that God's decree runs after this form, "I will predestinate Peter to salvation, *if* it should so happen that he doth believe and persevere;" but rather thus, "I do predestinate Peter to salvation, which, that he may infallibly obtain, I will give him both faith and perseverance." Were it otherwise, the foundation would not stand sure; yea, and God's gifts would not be without repentance, if God did not absolutely decree to give and bestow faith and perseverance to His elected ones. The covenant of grace runs in this tenure, "I will be a God to you, and ye shall be a people unto Me" that is, I will make ye so.

Inferences drawn from the foregoing:

1. A name written in Heaven, where no thief, no rust, no moth comes to destroy it, is better than to be enrolled in princely courts; 'tis a name better than of sons and daughters, to be a free citizen of Heaven.

2. Though we are changeable creatures, yet unchangeable

love is towards us, that keeps faster hold of us than we of it.

3. It is infinite condescension that the great God should hold a poor lump of clay so fast in His Almighty hands, as to secure our interest to all eternity.

John 10:28-29: And I give unto them eternal life; and they shall never perish, neither shall any [man] pluck them out of my hand. My Father, which gave [them] me, is greater than all; and no [man] is able to pluck [them] out of my Father's hand.

1 Peter 1:4-5: To an inheritance incorruptible, and undefiled, and that fadeth not away, reserved in heaven for you, Who are kept by the power of God through faith unto salvation ready to be revealed in the last time.

The Third Property of the Divine Decree;
It is ABSOLUTE

It is absolute in respect of the efficient impulsive cause which cannot be anything out of God, as the following reasons prove.

1. If the Divine decree be eternal it must be absolute; for nothing can be assigned before an eternal act, as the efficient cause of it. There cannot be a cause of the will of God out of God. Predestination is an immanent act of the Divine will; and so, not only the cause, but also the first cause of all created beings; and therefore cannot (in any good sense) be said to depend on foreseen transient acts in the creature; so, by consequence, must be an absolute act, unless we presume to make the volitions of God contingent upon the created and temporary volitions of man, which is grossly absurd. This goes to a denial of God being the first cause of all things.

2. *First*, if God be God; if He be an almighty, all wise, all free, and an all-disposing God, then His decree of Election must be absolute; for a conditional decree makes a conditional God, and plainly ungods Him, by ascribing such imperfections to Him

as are unworthy His majesty, and below His Divine being; as, first, it opposes His omnipotence—if some conditions be antecedent to the will of God, then the same are antecedent also to the power of God.

Second, it takes away the glory of the Divine wisdom in ordering all things; for if Peter must be willing to believe before God's decree concerning Peter, then Divine wisdom doth not determine the order of things.

Thirdly, it takes away the glory of God's absolute sovereign liberty and independence; for if Peter's believing and Judas' not believing be antecedent to the decree of God concerning them, then Peter and Judas make themselves the objects of election and non-election, and God hath not an absolute dominion over His own creatures. The potter hath not freedom to make this lump of clay a vessel of honour and that a vessel of dishonour, and the difference will arise more from the quality of the clay than the will of the potter, and God's will must be dependent on the will of man for its determinations. This plainly overthrows the independency of God.

Fourth, it takes away the glory of His all-disposing providence. If the decree be not absolute, how can God be said wholly to dispose of lots that are cast into the lap, as in Prv 16:33? Shall we say that the lot of the apostleship fell to Matthias by chance (Acts 1:26); was it not rather absolutely ordained and ordered by the Lord, to whom the Apostles prayed, as in Acts 1:24, saying, "Thou, Lord, which knoweth the hearts of all men, show whether (or which) of these two Thou has chosen... And they gave forth their lots; and the lot fell upon Matthias" (Acts 1:24,26)? Thus by the disposal of lots in the lap was Achan discovered to be Israel's curse, and Saul appointed to be Israel's king (Jos 7:14-18; 1Sa 10:19-21). Man purposeth, but God disposeth; because God by an absolute decree hath foreordained all things that do come to pass. They do not occur by random chance beyond God's intention; thus it is said, "It behoved Christ to suffer" (Lk 24:46).

3. If the will of the potter be an absolute will over his pots, much more is the will of God an absolute will over mankind. It is God's own comparison (Rom 9:20,21). God compares not Himself to a goldsmith, because a goldsmith hath costly materials, such as silver and gold, which lays some obligation on him to make honourable vessels therewith. But He compareth Himself to a potter, because first, the materials of a potter are vile and sordid, to wit, clay, so more answerable to fallen mankind, out of which God maketh His choice. We are not only clay (Job 4:19), but sinful clay through the fall. Second, the potter doth not make this difference among his pots for any foreseen inherent goodness in his clay (for the whole lump before him is of an equal temper and quality), but from the pleasure of His own will. Thus the potter's power over his materials is clearer from exception than that of the goldsmith, and illustrates more the absoluteness of God's will in His choice both in vessels of honour and vessels of dishonour. Again, the distance between the clay and potter is but a finite distance, even the distance only between one creature and another, animate and inanimate; but the distance between God and mankind is infinite, not only the natural distance between God and us, as we are creatures, but also the moral distance between us, as we are sinners. The potter also must have his clay made to his hand; he cannot make his own clay, though he may temper it for his work when he hath found it; but the great God creates His own clay. He created the earth out of which man was formed. "In the beginning God created the heaven and the earth" (Gn 1:1). "And the Lord God formed man of the dust of the ground" (Gn 2:7). It follows then, if the potter by an absolute will disposes of his pots, much more hath God a right concerning His creatures.

Inferences drawn from the preceding:

1. If the absolute will of God be the universal cause of all things, then no event can fall beyond or beside God's will; and chance (in the world's sense of it) is but the devil's blasphemous spit upon Divine providence.

2. God's absolute will cannot be resisted; as He hath willed, so shall it come to pass; and there is no hindering the execution of it. "The Lord of hosts hath sworn, saying, Surely as I have thought, so shall it come to pass; and as I have purposed, so shall it stand" (Isa 14:24). "Our God is in the Heavens: He hath done whatsoever He hath pleased" (Ps 115:3), "I know that Thou canst do everything" (Job 42:2).

3. Then let us learn submission to the will of God. Proud, yet brittle clay, will be knocking their sides against the absolute will of God, till they break in pieces; so did Adonijah, when Solomon must rule; compare 1Ki 1:5 with 1Ch 22:9, and mark the end of it, 1Ki 2:23-25. O for the grace of humility to enable us to adopt the language of the prophet,—

"Now, O Lord, Thou art our Father; we are the clay, and Thou our Potter, and we all are the work of Thy hand" (Isa 64:8).

The Fourth Property of the Divine Decree;
It is FREE

As the Divine decree is not conditional but absolute, so 'tis not of necessity but free, as flowing only from the pleasure of God's will. God is a free agent, and cannot fall under any obligation, so as to necessitate Him in any of His interactions with the creature; but He is graciously pleased of His own free love to oblige Himself.

1. The first argument to prove the freeness of the Divine decree is: such a decree as passeth without any obligation to necessitate the passing of it, must needs have the property of freeness; and thus it was with the divine decree. If there be any obligation it must be either in respect of objects or acts or motives; but God was not obliged in any of these respects.

First. He was not obliged in respect of objects, for God was under no necessity of having either any elect or any reprobate. He was happy in Himself from all eternity; would have been happy for ever without either of these; and to affirm that God stood in need of any such objects is to deny the perfections of God. If it is called humbling Himself to look down on things in Heaven, much more on things on earth.

Second. He was not obliged by acts, as acts are necessary by a moral obligation. God was under no moral obligation to man. He had done man no wrong if He had never willed man to be, much less to be holy and happy. God was not bound to any of His actions concerning man. He cannot be a debtor to many any other way than as He makes Himself a debtor of His own good pleasure. As in His promises His love moved Him to make them, and His truth binds Him to perform them, otherwise those actions would be actions of debt, and not acts of grace, contrary to the tenor of Scripture, which makes the whole work of man's salvation to flow wholly from the free grace of God.

Third. He was not obliged in respect to motives; neither in the creature, nor yet in Christ. Not in the creature, for the being of the creature (much more the faith and good works of the creature) was the effect of the decree of God, so could not be the motive of it. Nor could the Lord foresee repentance, faith, love etc., in the creature, antecedent to His own purpose in the gift of it. Neither is Christ Himself the moving cause of the Divine decree; for Christ is the effect of God's eternal love, not the cause of it. "God so loved the world that He gave His Son" (Jn 3:16). God's love gives Christ. Therefore we are said to be elected in Christ, but never for Christ; for Christ is an elect one Himself, as was shown before. Christ was first chosen, then the members. The love of God as immediately cometh from Himself to me, as to Christ; and He was foreordained to be our Head, and we to be His members. Thus we are Christ's; and Christ is God's as the effect of His love to His elect from all eternity (1 Cor 3:22).

2. The second argument to prove the freeness of Divine decree is taken from the testimony of the Word of God (the Bible) in which it is affirmed to be a free act, an act of grace and not of debt, an act of love and special favour, founded upon the mere good pleasure of God. "Even so, Father: for so it seemed good in

Thy sight" (Mt 11:26), "It is your Father's good pleasure to give you the kingdom" (Lk 12:32). It was a gracious purpose in God from all eternity (2 Tm 1:9; Eph 1:5,9,11). Paul's repeated exclamation is, "the pleasure of His own will," "the counsel of His own will;" but more fully in Rom 9:13,16 doth he exemplify this truth in Jacob and Esau. "Jacob have I loved, but Esau have I hated... It is not of him that willeth, nor of him that runneth, but of God that sheweth mercy." Both Malachi the Prophet (Mal 1:3), and Paul the Apostle make this instance of Jacob and Esau the fullest exemplification of free election. For they lay together in the same womb, and were born at the same time (for Jacob took hold of Esau's heel), so the contrary destinies of these two doth more illustrate the free predestination of God than any other two whatsoever. Of Jacob there came a distinguished people from all the world, even a Church unto God; and of Esau there sprang forth a persecuting seed. God hath no regard to faith in the one, or of infidelity in the other. When God's oracle passed upon them, they were both in their mother's womb, conceived in sin; and, if there were any pre-eminence, Esau had it, as being the first-born. What then determines the different outcomes? Nothing but the good pleasure of God. God will "have mercy on whom He will have mercy, and whom He will He hardeneth" (Rom 9:18). Now, in opposition to this carnal reason saith, "It was because God foresaw what they would do." Nay, but God loved them because He loved them (Dt 7:7,8). It was choosing love that He bare to them, and that is the best of the kind. That is the favour which God bears to His people: He loved them, and chose them for His own.

3. The third reason to prove the freeness of the Divine decree is: God hath in all ages given us examples of His free receiving some of mankind and rejecting others; this is plain from Scripture history. Of Adam's three sons, Cain, Abel, Seth, the eldest was rejected. Of Noah's three, Japheth, Shem and Ham, the youngest was rejected. Of Terah's three, Abraham, Nahor, Haran, the middlemost was rejected; for Nahor was an idolater,

and Laban sware by Nahor's idol (compare Gn 31:53 with Jos 24:2). Now why this picking and choosing, this receiving and rejecting; eldest at one time, youngest at another time, and middlemost at a third time? What is all this but to show that neither birth nor age, nor anything foreseen or existing in the creature, can produce any claim, but that all lies in the free election of God! We can give no reason, save the good pleasure of God, why Pharaoh and Nebuchadnezzar (both engaged in the same warfare against Israel, the church of God) had different dispensations of Heaven upon them; the one was hardened and the other humbled; why Pharaoh's baker was hanged and his butler restored to his office again; why two men shall be in one bed, the one taken, the other justified; why two women shall be grinding at one mill, the one taken, the other justified; why Aaron's rod, of all twelve, only blossomed.

4. *First*,—If the fruits of the Divine decree be free, then must the decree itself be free. This assumption is clear, for first, our calling is from free love. Christ freely, and of His own sovereign will, called James and John, the two sons of Zebedee, and justify their father uncalled with the hired servants (Mr 1:20). "He called unto Him whom He would" (Mr 3:13). "It is given unto you to know the mysteries of the kingdom of Heaven, but to them it is not given" (Mt 13:11). "We know that the Son of God is come, and hath given us an understanding, that we may know Him that is true" (1 Jn 5:20). "Thou hast hid these things from the wise and prudent, and hast revealed them unto babes. Even so, Father: for so it seemed good in Thy sight" (Mt 11:26).

Second, our sanctification is from free grace. Of His own will He begat us (Jas 1:18). The sanctifying grace breathes where it listeth; and the wind at sea, is as much at our command as the fresh gales of this renewing Spirit.

Third, our glorification is free. Eternal life is the gift of God (Rom 6:23); He doth not sell it for foreseen faith or works, but He freely gives it. Now if all these fruits of election be free, then the election itself to these fruits must be free also. If faith be the free gift of God (Eph 2:8), then predestination to faith must of necessity be also free, for God worketh all things according to the counsel of His own will (Eph 1:11).

Christian, there is much comfort and establishment to be drawn from a view of the freeness of the grace of God; then:

1. Admire free grace in this decree of predestination, and cry, How is it, Lord, that Thou dost manifest Thyself and Thy love to me, and not unto the world (Jn 14:22)?

2. Thou makest not thyself to differ from others, but free grace does it for thee. Thou art a lump of clay in the hands of the potter, no better than others; yea, pressed down to hell by Adam's fall; that God should lift thee up to Heaven, be thankful.

3. Rejoice in the Lord, sing to the honour of His great name, and live to His praise and glory. Did David dance before the Lord with all his might? Did he say to Michal, "It was before the Lord, who chose me before your father, to appoint me ruler over ...Israel; therefore will I play before the Lord" (2 Sm 6:14,21)? David's appointment, at that time, was but to an earthly kingdom; thou art freely chosen to inherit an Heavenly: therefore I say rejoice.

The Fifth Property of the Divine Decree;
It is DISCRIMINATING

That it is discriminating and particular, not universal or general, may be proved from the following arguments:

1. The very word used, *Election*, confutes the universality of it. There can be no choice made, where all are taken, and none justified. That cannot be called election which is equally extended to every individual. He doth not elect that doth not prefer some before others. God did not choose all the thirty-two thousand Israelites that were with Gideon, to save Israel by, out of the hand of Midian, but only the three hundred that lapped; and

these were chosen from out of the thirty and two thousand (Jud 7:3-7). God did not choose all the nations, but only Israel, to be a special people to Himself, "Thy God hath chosen thee...above all people that are upon the face of the earth" (Dt 7:6). Election must therefore be discriminating, and a making of some to differ from others.

2. Scripture expressly states that only *few are chosen*, though many be called (Mt 20:16). It is only a little flock (Lk 12:32), and but one from a city and two from a family that are brought to Zion (Jer 3:14). "I have chosen you out of the world," saith Christ (Jn 15:19); and the Lord calls Paul a chosen vessel unto Him (Acts 9:15; 22:14). How ill it sounds in the ears of a gospel-spirit to say that Pharaoh and Judas were elected as well as Paul and Barnabas; and that Simon Magus was elected as well as Simon Peter; all which a general election, which is the Arminian hypothesis, most necessarily asserts. How can these "reprobate silver" pieces be, in a gospel sense, termed chosen vessels (as Paul was) to know God's will, and to see the Just One (Acts 22:14)?

3. If election be general under a condition of believing, then Pilate, Caiaphas, and Judas were elected under that condition; and so God is brought in to speak after this manner: I have appointed to save Pilate, Caiaphas and Judas if they will believe in the death of Christ; but, if they believe, Christ shall not be crucified, for those are the very men appointed by My determinate counsel to put Christ to death (see Acts 2:23; 4:28). Had these men believed (and they have believed according to the Arminians' views), then God's decree concerning Christ's death would not have been absolute, but depending on a condition which those men might have fulfilled (namely,—believing in Christ's death), which had they done, they had believed in that which then never would have come to pass. Thus carnal reason besmirches Divine wisdom!

4. How can it be rightly said that God ever intended the salvation of any others, except those who are, or shall be, effectually saved? This would frustrate the will of God, even His will of intention, and would be contrary to the following scriptures, "Our God...hath done whatsoever He hath pleased" (Ps 115:3). "I know that Thou canst do everything, and that no thought can be withholden from Thee" (Job 42:2). And no man can resist the will of God, for He will have mercy on whom He will have mercy, and whom He will He hardeneth. And, if after all, O vain man! thou wilt still object, and say, "Why doth He yet find fault? for who hath resisted His will?" the only answer for thee is, "Nay but, O man, who art thou that repliest against God? Shall the thing formed say to Him that formed it, Why hast thou made me thus?" (Rom 9:19). Thus it was, according to the sovereign will of Jehovah, that Jacob and Esau were discriminated the one from the other.

5. The apostle shows that there is this discriminating difference between man and man, that some are chosen to life, and therefore shall most certainly obtain it! Others are refused and remain in a perishing condition, which they shall certainly not escape. "The election hath obtained it, and the rest were blinded" (Rom 11:7). The difference is of God, according to the purpose of election; not as of Him that foresees faith or works, but as of Him that *gives* both.

We may learn from the preceding:

1. It is distinguishing love that our Potter hath made us what we are, men and women. All creatures, even toads and other baser animals, were formed of the same dust with man. "The Lord God formed man of the dust of the ground" (Gn 2:7); "and out of the ground the Lord God formed every beast" (Gn 2:19).

2. It is the will of God that some be poor and others rich; so here, that some be vessels of honour, and others of dishonour.

3. Christ raised not all up that were dead, but Lazarus, etc.,

nor all that were born blind, but him mentioned in John 9. Bless God for raising thee up from thy death of sin, and healing thy blindness, and not others! Thou wert alike undeserving with them! Thou wert, thou art still, in thyself, a sinner! And if thou art taught by grace, the last words on thy faltering tongue will be the publican's prayer: "*God be merciful to me a sinner.*"

The Sixth and last Property of the Divine Decree; *It is EXTENSIVE*

The Divine decree of God's electing and predestinating love, although discriminating and particular, is, nevertheless, very extensive— "I beheld, and lo, a great multitude, which no man could number, of all nations, and kindreds, and people, and tongues, stood before the throne, and before the Lamb... and cried with a loud voice, saying *Salvation* to our God which sitteth upon the throne, and unto the Lamb." (Re 7:9). There is a general decree that relates to all created beings, both animate and inanimate, celestial and terrestrial; and extends itself to every individual in the whole creation of God. For as it gave a being to all things, so it preserves them in that being while they continue in the world; and the work of Providence, which extends itself from angels to worms, succeeds the work of creation. Now although this special Divine decree of predestination extends not (as the general decree) to every individual, it is nevertheless very extensive, even to all ranks, sexes, ages, nations and generations.

1. *To all ranks.* To all sorts and ranks of men, to princes and peasants, to high and low, to rich and poor, to bond and free. It extends itself to kings, for among them hath God His chosen vessels—His Davids, His Solomons, His Hezekiahs, His Mannassehs. Though the Scriptures say (1 Cor 1:26) "Not many mighty, not many noble, are called," yet it doth not say, not any; for God hath had some great ones to own His ways in all ages. It extends to servants also (Titus 2:9,11), for God bestows His love

on those in rags as well as those in robes. The poor have the gospel preached unto them (Mt 11:5), and God is no respecter of persons.

2. *To all sexes.* To both sexes is the decree extended, to male and female. God hath His elect ladies. "The elder unto the elect lady and her children, whom I love in the truth;" and "The children of thy elect sister, greet thee" (2Jo 1:13), and both male and female are one in Christ Jesus (Ga 3:28) "I entreat thee also, true yoke-fellow, help those women, which laboured with me in the gospel...whose names are in the book of life" (Phm 4:3).

3. *To all ages.* To young and old, to children, and to those of riper years; yea, very infants lay in the womb of the eternal decree, before ever they came out of their mother's womb. "Before I formed thee in the belly I knew thee; and before thou camest forth out of the womb I sanctified thee; and I ordained thee a prophet unto the nations:" (Jer 1:5). John the Baptist was filled with the Holy Ghost, even from the womb (Lk 1:15); and it is probable David believed that his child belonged to the election of grace, and that its soul was bound up in the bundle of life; for he comforted himself thus; "I shall go to him, but he shall not return to me" (2 Sm 12:23). David's going to the grave could yield him but little comfort.

4. *To all nations.* Grace is not confined within the walls of one nation only, but is extended to Jew and Gentile, to circumcision and uncircumcision, to Barbarian and Scythian, bond and free (Col 3:11), to some of every nation under Heaven (Acts 2:5). The partition wall, which seperated Jew from Gentile, is thrown down. Our Lord saith, "and other sheep I have which are not of this (the Jewish) fold: them also I must bring" (Jn 10:16). This predestinating love effectually calls its chosen ones from all quarters. "I have loved thee; therefore, I will bring thy seed from the east, and gather thee from the west; I will say to the north, Give up: and to the south, Keep not back; bring My sons

from afar, and My daughters from the ends of the earth; Even everyone that is called by My name" (Isa 43:4-7).

5. *To all generations.* Predestinating love is like a river that runs underground, and breaks out in certain places above the earth. To this river, this ocean of everlasting love, Moses had his eye, when of Joseph he said, "Blessed of the Lord be his land... for the deep that coucheth beneath" (Dt 33:13). So fresh veins of election breaketh forth, sometimes in one generation, and sometimes in another. It is not bound up as to time -- neither before the law, nor under the law, nor after the law; but, in every generation God hath His Church visible on the earth, and the gates of hell cannot prevail against it. As God is no respecter of persons, so neither is He of places, nations, or generations; but hath had, and He will have, His hidden ones to the world's end.

O believer! there is ground for much rejoicing, and strong consolation, in a view of the extensiveness of God's everlasting love.

1. If predestinating love extends itself to all degrees, then, they which are poor of wealth may be rich in faith, and a master's servant may be the Lord's freeman.

2. If to both sexes, then the weaker vessel may be a chosen vessel, and an heir of the grace of life.

3. If to all ages, then believing parents may have hope of their dying children; they may belong to the election of grace; they may be bound up in the swaddling bands of the covenant of grace; so they are not as without hope for them.

4. If to all nations, then the ends of the earth may look towards Christ (as He is lifted up on the pole of the everlasting Gospel) and be saved (Isa 45:22).

5. If to all generations, then predestinating love is an inexhaustible fountain! crying always, "Is there yet any of the house of the Lord among mankind that I may shew the kindness of God unto?" (2 Sm 9:3)

Of Conditional Predestination

Having stated the doctrine of Divine predestination, as revealed in the Scriptures, and having, from the same source, proved that it is possessed of various distinguishing properties, such as eternal, unchangeable, absolute, free, discriminating, and extensive; I come now, secondly, to consider the Arminians' view of it, viz.: "That it is conditional, upon the foresight of faith, works, perseverance," etc.

To this I answer, that predestination cannot be conditional, upon a foresight of man's faith, works, or perseverance, etc., because of the twelve following reasons:

1. That which the Scriptures declare to be the cause and ground of our election, that, and that only, must be the cause and ground of it.

The good pleasure of God is the only cause and ground of our election, not any foresight of our faith, etc. That the Scriptures declare this, appears plain from Eph 1:5; "According to the good pleasure of His will," and from Eph 1:9 "Having made known to us the mystery of His will, according to His good pleasure;" and, "predestinated according to the purpose of Him who worketh all things after the counsel of His own will." Also, from Mt 11:25,26: "Thou hast hid these things from the wise and prudent, and hast revealed them unto babes." But why so? It is "Even so, Father: for so it seemed good in Thy sight." Again the Scriptures fully declare the same truth in Rom 9:11-15, and Rom 11:5; and in 2 Tm 1:9, our salvation and calling is stated to be, "not according to our works, but according to His own purpose and grace, which was given us in Christ Jesus before the world began." The time would fail me in enumerating more passages of Scripture, for the whole Bible as with one voice crieth aloud, election is of sovereign grace and not of works; flowing only from the absolute will and good pleasure of God.

2. That which makes election an action of debt ought not to be received; and the conditional decree doth this.

An action of grace, and an action of debt, are contradictory terms. If election be an act of grace (and the whole work of salvation hath been proved to be wholly and solely from free grace), then 'tis abominable and to be rejected to make it an act of debt. If the decree be conditional (upon foreseen faith and perseverance), then is it an act of debt and not of grace, an act of justice and not of mercy. For a decree of giving glory to believers persevering, as their reward, can be nothing else but remunerative justice.

3. That which makes God go out of Himself, in His immanent and eternal actings, ought not to be received; and the conditional decree doth so.

It makes God look upon this or that in the creature upon which the will of God is determined; thus man is the author of his own salvation, and God is not the author of it. The doctrine of the conditional decree sets God upon His watch-tower of foreknowledge to espy what men will do; whether they will believe or not, obey or not, persevere or not, and according to His observation of their actings, so He determines His will concerning them; thus the perfection both of the Divine knowledge and Divine will is with one breath denied.

4. No temporal thing can be the efficient cause of our eternal election; but faith, obedience, etc., are temporal things, the former being wrought in us, and the latter performed by us, in their appointed time.

What is this but to prefer time before eternity, and to set up a post-destination instead of a predestination?

5. That which is the fruit and effect of the Divine decree cannot be the cause of it; and faith, perseverance, etc., are but the fruits and effects of electing love.

Such as are given to Christ in the decree of election, do come to, or believe in Christ; others do not come, do not believe; and the cause assigned is, because they are not of His sheep, because they are not given to Him. "All that the Father giveth Me shall come to Me" (Jn 6:37). Coming to Christ is believing on Him. "Ye believe not, because ye are not of My sheep" (Jn 10:26). "As many as were ordained to eternal life believed"* (Acts 13:48). We may not (according to the Arminian notion) read it, "as many as believed were ordained unto life;" for this would be setting the cart before the horse, as if the means were ordained before the end. We are predestinated that we should be holy, not because we are holy (Eph 1:4). We are foreordained to walk in good works, not because we do so (Eph 2:10). We are predestinated to be conformed to the image of Christ, not because we are so (Rom 8:29). It is the election that obtains faith, and not faith that obtains election (Rom 11:7). And the Apostle, in 2 Tm 1:9, excludes all works (both foreseen and existing), showing that God's gracious purpose is the original of all. Yea, Paul himself was chosen that he might know the will of God, not that he was foreseen to do so (Acts 22:14); and he tells the Thessalonians, that "God hath from the beginning chosen you to salvation through sanctification of the Spirit and belief of the truth" (2 Thes 2:13). We may not make that an antecedent to election which is but the consequent of it. "I have chosen you, and ordained you, that ye should go and bring forth fruit" (Jn 15:16).

6. That which sets up an inferior cause before a superior ought not be admitted, and the conditional decree doth so.

God is the cause of causes, and the first cause of all things. There can be no being but from Him, there can be nothing before Him. "Of Him, and through Him, and to Him, are all things" (Rom 11:36). "In Him we live, and move, and have our

---

*Acts 13:48, "Therefore either all were not appointed to everlasting life, or else all should have believed; but because that is not so, it followeth that some certain were ordained: and therefore God did not only foreknow, but also fore-ordained, that either faith, nor the effects of faith should be the cause of his ordaining or appointment, but his ordaining should be the cause of faith." —Beza

being" (Acts 17:28). O Lord, "Thou hast created all things, and for Thy pleasure they are and were created" (Re 4:11). God is the chief efficient cause, and the ultimate end of all beings; but if any being be antecedent to the determinations of God's will, this would take away the dignity of the supreme cause, and make an act of man superior to that of God.

7. That which takes away the certainty and unchangeableness of the Divine decree ought not to be received, and the conditional decree doth so.

If anything in man move God to choose man, then the purpose of God cannot remain firm, but must depend on some contingent act in man, be it faith, works or perseverance. If it depends on our persevering in faith, it cannot be firm and certain, according to the Arminian doctrine of falling away. For the Arminian hypothesis states the decree of God after this changeable dress, viz., "I will save all if they will obey Me; but I see they will sin. I must permit them, but I will condemn them all; yet this decree of condemnation shall not be peremptory. I will send Christ to redeem all, to save all again, if they will believe; but I see they will not. I will decree to save such as I foresee will believe, and persevere in believing." Oh what a changeable picture of an unchangeable God!

8. That which makes us to choose God, before God chooses us, ought not to be received; and the conditional decree upon faith foreseen doth so.

If God does not choose us until faith is foreseen in us, then it necessarily follows that we choose God before He chooses us, and we love Him before He loves us, contrary to these scriptures, "Ye have not chose Me, but I have chosen you" (Jn 15:16). "We love Him, because He first loved us" (1 Jn 4:19). But the Arminians go further still, for they say, "We must be foreseen, not only to believe, but also to persevere in believing;" that is, not only to choose God for our God, but also to continue in that choice to the last moment of our existence before we can be fit objects of God's choice or election!

9. That which taketh away the mysteriousness of the Divine decree ought to be rejected, and this doctrine of foreseen faith doth so.

It is a dangerous presumption for men to take upon themselves, with unwashed hands, to unriddle the deep mysteries* of God with their carnal reason; where the great apostle stands at the gaze, crying, "O the depth, how unsearchable!" and "Who knoweth the mind of the Lord!" Had Paul been of the Arminian persuasion he would have answered, "Those are elected that are foreseen to believe and persevere!" This answer would not have been hard to understand even by the unlearned (that is, the carnal) men of the world, who "wrest the Scriptures unto their own destruction" (2 Pt 3:16). But Paul was ignorant, and these men are wiser than the Holy Ghost; for he tells us that our election proceedeth from the will of the Elector, and not from anything in the elected. The sovereign will of God is the supreme rule of all righteousness; He will have "mercy on whom He will have mercy, and whom He will He hardeneth" (Rom 9:18). Had foreseen faith and perseverance been the causes and conditions of election, there had been no mystery in it.

10. That election which is shadowed out to us in God's love to Jacob (both person and nation) is the election according to truth; but that election was not upon foreseen faith or works.

First, Jacob the person. He was under electing love; all foresight of faith and works being excluded. "Jacob have I loved" (Rom 9:12,13). To love Jacob is to will unto him the greatest

---

* Dear Reader! If thou art a child of God! I then desire thee to pause, with me, at this word, *mysteries*. The mystery of his will! The wisdom of God in a mystery! The great mystery of godliness! Truly, truly (as Master Ness hath here observed), it is a dangerous presumption for men to take upon them with unwashed hands to unriddle the deep mysteries of God, with their carnal reason. Alas! proud man is ofttimes vainly puffed up by his fleshly mind, disdaining to remain ignorant of that, concerning the INFINITE JEHOVAH himself, which it is impossible, in the nature of things, he should ever attain to the knowledge of, in this world. Vain man would be wise, though man be born like a wild ass's colt, Job 11:12. It is said, the Lord knoweth vain men

good, even everlasting salvation, and all things which accompany the same. And this was before there was any difference between him and Esau, for they were both alike in the womb, both conceived in sin. "For the children being not yet born, neither having done any good or evil, that the purpose of God according to election might stand, not of works, but of him that calleth; It was said unto her, The elder shall serve the younger" (Rom 9:11,12).

Second, Jacob, the nation. Our Election is typified by God's election of Israel, which plainly appears not to be an election upon foresight of worthiness in Israel; "Not for thy righteousness, or for the uprightness of thine heart... Understand therefore, that the Lord thy God giveth thee not this good land to possess it for thy righteousness; for thou art a stiffnecked people" (Dt 9:5,6). All works and worthiness are excluded, and the reason assigned is, "Because the Lord loved you" (Dt 7:8).

11. That which sets up the rotten Dagon of man's free-will, before or above the ark of God's special predestinating grace, ought to be rejected; and the conditional decree doth so.

The conditional decree is grounded upon a foresight of our wills receiving or rejecting of proposed grace; and so man's will is made the first mover and advanced above God's will. And the act of predestination is put in the will and power of the predestinated, and not in that of the Divine Predestinator. Hereby the power of ordering man's salvation is wrested (as it were) out of

---

(ver.11). He doth indeed know them. He knoweth that they and theirs are VANITY. They would in the strength of their own wisdom, and of their own carnal search, find out God; yet are too proud to take the Scriptures of Truth for their guide. Listen, vain man, listen to the challenges, and the all-important questions of the infinite JEHOVAH to the worm Job (chapters 38, 39, 40, 41), and may the Lord enable thee to wrap they face in the mantle of thine own nothingness; and, taking up Job's reply, to say, "I have uttered that I understood not; things too wonderful for me, which I know not. I have heard of thee by the hearing of the ear, but now mine eye seeth thee, therefor *I abhor myself*, and repent in dust and ashes."

God's hands, and put into the hands of our free-will. Then salvation is the work of the saved, and not of the saver; and to will and to do is not of God's good pleasure (Php 2:13). Thus men wickedly think that God is such an one as themselves (Ps 50:21), wavering and fluctuating in His counsels and hanging in pendulous suspenses; yea, taking up new consultations, as dependent on the will of men, and the contingent acts flowing therefrom.

12. That which infers a succession of acts in God ought not to be admitted, and election upon foresight doth so.

God is one act, and in Him there can be no succession, for then He would not be "I AM." Foresight of faith necessarily presupposes a foregoing decree concerning the being of that faith foreseen. For, first, God must decree faith to be; second, He foresees that faith; third, then decrees to save upon that foresight. So that this foresight necessarily comes between two decrees.

Much more might be added, such as — foreseen faith can have no place in dying infants, yet of such is the kingdom of Heaven, and their names are written in the book of life (see Re 20:12). But to sum up the whole in one sentence: A conditional decree makes a conditional God, since the decree is God Himself decreeing. Therefore it must be rejected.

> "May not the Sovereign Lord on high
> Dispense His favours as He will;
> Choose some to life, while others die,
> And yet be just and gracious still?
>
> Shall man reply against the Lord,
> And call his Maker's ways unjust?
> The thunder of whose dreadful word
> Can crush a thousand worlds to dust.
>
> But, O my soul, if truths so bright
> Should dazzle and confound thy sight,
> Yet still His written will obey,
> And wait the great decisive day!"

Objections Against the Absolute Decree of Predestination Answered

I have stated and proved the doctrine of absolute Divine Predestination. I have also considered, and, I trust, scripturally refuted the Arminian's notion of it, that it is conditional. I shall now, thirdly, answer a few of the principal objections brought by them against this Divine absolute decree of unconditional predestination. The Arminians deal with this doctrine as the heathen emperors did with primitive Christians in the ten first persecutions, who wrapped them up in the skins of beasts, and then exposed them to be torn to pieces by fierce dogs; so do the Arminians with this great truth. They first dress it up in an ugly shape, with their own false glosses upon it, and then they let fly at it one cynical sarcasm after another, saying, "This doctrine of absolute predestination goes to accuse and charge God with injustice, dissimulation, hypocrisy," etc.

Objection 1

Of injustice, in giving to equal persons unequal things; contrary to that scripture which saith, "that God is no respecter of persons" (Acts 10:34).

Answer:

1. This was objected against Paul's doctrine, "What shall we say then? is there unrighteousness (is there injustice) with God? God forbid" (Rom 9:14). And seeing the apostle brings it in as the cavil of carnal reason against God's decree, we have therefore sufficient ground to reject it. God must not lose the honour of His righteousness, because the reason of it appears not to our shallow understandings. We may not reprehend what we cannot comprehend. The justice of God must not be measured by the standard of our reason; what is this but speaking wickedly for God, and talking deceitfully for Him (Job 13:7), and plainly robbing Him of all righteousness that is not consonant with our model? The work of God, and the wisdom of God, must ever be viewed as inseparably united.

2. God is righteousness itself; and darkness may sooner come from the sun (which is the fountain and source of light) than any unrighteous act from God. God's ways are always equal, though men think otherwise of them. "Yet ye say, The way of the Lord is not equal. Hear now, O house of Israel; Is not My way equal? are not your ways unequal?" (Eze 18:25); and though they be sometimes secret and past finding out (Rom 11:33), yet are they always just. God's will is the rule ruling; but not as regulated by man's depraved reason. God is the origin of all good; He is also the Foundation of justice and equity. God is too kind to do us harm, and too just to do us wrong.

3. Jacob and Esau were equal in the womb, yet had an unequal disposing decree concerning them; this was God's right and power to do. This the apostle demonstrates, first, from Moses' testimony, "I will make all My goodness pass before thee, and I will proclaim the name of the Lord before thee, and will be gracious to whom I will be gracious, and I will show mercy on whom I will show mercy" (Ex 33:19). It is His right to do so. And, secondly, from the example of the potter, who hath power over his pots, yet less than God over His creatures. Now that which the pot cannot do with the potter, that man may not do with his Maker. But the pot (supposing it could speak) could not blame the potter of injustice in appointing equal lumps to unequal ends.

4. God's decree is not an act of injustice, but of lordship and sovereignty. Justice always presupposes debt; but God (who was perfect in Himself from all eternity) could not be a debtor to man, who had his all from God; the decree is not a matter of right and wrong, but of free favour, Grace is God's own, He may do what He will with it. "Is it not lawful for Me to do what I will with Mine own? Is thine eye evil, because I am good?" (Mt 20:15). If He gives grace to some and not to others, it is no wrong in Him that is not bound to give to any.

5. God is not a respecter of persons, because He doth not choose men for their works' sake. It was before Jacob and Esau had done either good or evil. He finds all alike, and nothing to

cast the balance of His choice but His own mere good pleasure. God is a free agent, and under no law in giving grace.

Objection 2
Of cruelty; as if God were worse to His creatures than tigers to their young: than rat-catchers who stop up all holes, and then hunt them with their dogs, etc.*

Answer:
1. This is charging God foolishly, seeing no act of God can be a means to damn men. Men's own acts are the cause of it; to wit, the fulfilling their own lusts. As reprobation gives not such a grace as infallibly to make them better, so it works nothing in them by which they are made worse.

2. 'Tis a mere fallacy: as if the decree of non-election was the procuring cause of man's damnation. Sin is the cause of damnation, but reprobation is not the cause of sin. David's order to Solomon concerning Joab and Shimei was not the cause why either the one or the other came to an untimely end; but it was treason against Solomon in Joab, and running from Jerusalem in Shimei, which procured their deaths (see 1Ki 2:5, 28, 40, 42).

3. It is a false hypothesis to suppose that God, in the decree of reprobation, doth by an effectual means intend to bring men to damnation as in the decree of election to bring others to salvation: for salvation is a favour not due any, so God may absolutely give or deny it; but damnation is a punishment, so hath relation to a fault. Means to salvation is the gift of free grace,

---

* There was a favourite objection usually urged by the late Mr. Wesley, against the Sovereignty of God, who compared the doctrine of absolute Predestination, to that of casting a man bound into the midst of a house, setting that house on fire, and then calling out to the man to escape for his life: "I would gladly, but cannot, cries the man, for I am bound." Is not this specious argument *completely answered* in the replies to objections 2 and 3? Dear Reader! May the Lord give thee well to ponder on these replies. May the Lord anoint thine eyes with eye salve! The doctrine of the *freedom*

but damnation comes of man's own voluntary sin, and is the fruit or wages of it. "The wages of sin is death; but the gift of God is eternal life through Jesus Christ our Lord" (Rom 6:23). It is God that fitteth Peter for salvation; but Judas fits himself for damnation.

4. Should God constrain the creature to sin, and then damn him for it, He delighteth in the destruction of His creature, contrary to Eze 13:23 and 23:11. God did not thrust Adam into his sin, as, after he had willingly sinned, He thrust him out of Paradise. Man's punishment is from God as a judge; but man's destruction is from himself as a sinner. Let it be repeated, and again repeated, that man's sin came freely from himself.

Objection 3

It is objected against the absolute decree, that it makes God guilty of dissimulation in calling upon such as are under the negative part of it to repent, etc., just as if God bid men, whose eyes He had closed, to judge of colours; or those whose feet He had bound, to rise up and walk.

Answer:

1. The non-elect's not repenting is not only from want of power ["No man can come to Me, except the Father... draw him" (Jn 6:44)]; but also from want of will, "Ye will not come to Me, that ye might have life" (Jn 5:40). None are damned because they can do no better, but because they will do no better. If there were no will there would be no hell: and this will be the very hell of hells, that men have been, felo de se, self destroyers.

---

of the will is an all-important point. It appeareth to me, that these pages (48 to 56) contain the cream, yea, the very marrow of the book. Here it all hinges. It is—who shall be the Lord and Master? God or man? Who shall be on the throne? God or man? O the folly, the folly of abominable and filthy man, who drinketh inquity like water, to stretch out his hand against God; to strengthen himself against the Almighty: to run upon Him, even on his neck, upon the thick bosses of His bucklers, Job 15:26.

2. Man had a power in Adam. God gave him knowledge in his understanding, rectitude in his will, and purity in his affections: these were all lost by the Fall. God must not lose His authority to command because man due to of sin hath lost his ability to obey.

3. May it not more truly be said, that it is the Arminians who charge God with folly and dissimulation, by their representing Him as disappointed in his purpose, and by their bringing Him in as speaking thus: "I do indeed earnestly desire to save you, but ye so hinder that I cannot do what I desire; I would, if ye would: therefore since I am, by you, frustrated of My intention, I will change My purpose of saving you, and My consequent will shall be determination to destroy you?" So said Vorstius the Arminian, "Things may happen that may bring God to grief, having tried all things in vain!"

4. But there is another view to be taken here. When God giveth command to spiritual acts He grants power to obey them. So it was when Christ bade the man to stretch out the withered hand, and Lazarus to come forth out of the grave. The call and command of God is the conduit-pipe of strength and ability.

Objection 4
God's decree cannot be absolute and infallible, because it might have been frustrated by the possibility of Adam's standing.

Answer:
1. Adam's standing was possible respecting himself, but not respecting God. To say that Adam might not have sinned is a categorical and simple proposition, and will hold good, Adam being considered in himself as clothed with the freedom of his will; and to say also, that it could not be but that Adam would sin is equally true, considering Adam was subordinate to the decree of God, determining what Adam would do out of the freedom of his own will.

2. As it respects man, Adam might have stood as well as fallen; for God gave not His creature a law only, but also furnished him with power sufficient to keep that law if he would; and if man had not been mutable, he had been God and not

man. Man is mutable; God alone is immutable; in this He, the Lord, is distinguished from all created beings. Yet as it respects God, it was not possible man should stand; for in God's decree it was certain that man, being left to the mutability of his own will (upon Satan's tempting and God's permitting), would voluntarily incline to evil. Therefore Adam sinned freely in respect of himself, but necessarily in respect of God. He acted as freely therein as if there had been no decree, and yet as infallibly as if there had been no liberty. God's decree took not away man's liberty; man in the Fall, while fulfilling the decree of God, yet freely exercised the proper motions of his will.

3. Thus then God, by decreeing Adam's sin, did not subtract from Adam any grace that he had; for He decreed that he should sin voluntarily. He diminished not that power with which he was endued, only He superadded not that grace by which Adam would infallibly not have fallen; which grace was no way due to man, neither was God bound to bestow it on him. So that Adam might stand, in respect of himself; yet certainly fall, in respect of God. The Jews might have broken Christ's bones, in respect of their own free-will in such actions, yet was it not possible they should do so; for "A bone of Him shall not be broken" (Jn 19:36). It was possible, in a sense, that Christ should be delivered from His passion by legions of angels (Mt 26:53), "But how then shall the scriptures be fulfilled, that thus it must be?" (Mt 26:54). It was possible, in respect of the thing, that God might have pardoned sinners without a Christ; but impossible, inasmuch as God had decreed Christ to be the ransom. To argue on the Arminian hypothesis of free-will, 'tis possible none may be saved or none lost; and then either Heaven or hell would be superfluous.

Supra and Sub-lapsarianism, the difference between stated:

Objection 5
The predestinarians cannot agree about stating their decree; some stating it before the Fall, as the supra-lapsarians; and others after the Fall, as the sub-lapsarians.

Answer:

1. The Arminians, by the law of retaliation, may be called sub-mortuarians, for their holding no full election till men die; and post-destinarians, for placing the eternal decree behind the race of man's life. Surely when believers die they are the subjects of glorification, not of election. Christ should have said (upon this hypothesis) to the penitent thief, "This day thou shalt be fully elected," not, "Thou shalt be with me in Paradise." And may they not also be styled re-lapsarians, for saying that the elect may totally and finally fall away; and that he who is a child of God today may be a child of the devil tomorrow?

2. Those notions of sub and supra are but human conceptions of the order of the Divine decree, which so far transcends our understanding, that our weak capacities cannot comprehend it but after the manner of men. Those several states of man, before and after the Fall, are not in the Divine understanding as they are in ours, by a succession of acts, one after another; but God by one single act orders all things; and the Divine idea in the decree is a representative of all those states at once. They are not sub-ordinanda but co-ordinanda; not this after that, but altogether in one instant of eternity.*

---

* Supra-lapsarians and Sub-lapsarians.—It hath been a question in the Church, " Whether men were considered, in the mind of God, in the decree of election, as fallen or tinfallen; as in the corrupt mass, through the fall; or in the pure mass of creatureship, previous to it, and as to be created. There are some that think the Latter, So considered, were the objects of election in the divine mind; who are called supra-lapsarians: On the other hand there are those, whose minds lead them to adopt the Former, who are stiled sublapsarians, and these are for men being considered as created and fallen, in the decree of election. The arguments used on both sides are many; but the Difference is not so great as may be thought at first sight; for BOTH AGREE In The MAIN, AND MATERIAL THINGS, IN THE DOCTRINE OF Election. As—1, That it is personal and particular; is of persons by name, whose names are written in the Lamb's book of life.'—

Objection 6

Absolute election makes men remiss in duty; saying, "What need or use is there of good works? Let me live as I list; if I am elected to salvation I shall certainly be saved."

Answer:

1. God's decree establishes means; it doth not only ordain the end, but the means to that end; and the one is never separated from the other. God decrees that the earth shall be fruitful; this doth not exclude, but includes, that the sun must shine upon it, showers must water it, and the husbandman must till it, as his God instructs him (Isa 28:26). God decrees that fifteen years shall be added to Hezekiah's life; this made him neither careless of his health nor negligent of his food; he said not, "Though I run into fire, or into the water, or drink poison, I shall nevertheless live so long;" but natural providence, in the due use of means, co-wrought so as to bring him on to that period of time pre-ordained for him. Man's industry is subservient to God's decree; it is called, "the life of thine hand" (Isa 57:10). We may not tempt the Lord our God.

2. The golden chain has so linked the means to the end, and sanctification in order to salvation, that God doth infallibly stir up the elect to the use of the means, as well as bring them to the end by the means. "Brethren beloved of the Lord, God hath from the beginning chosen you to salvation, through sanctification of

---

2. That it is absolute and unconditional, not depending on the will of-men, nor on any thing to be done by the creature.—3. That it is wholly owing to the will and pleasure of God; and not to the faith, holiness, obedience, and good works of men; nor to a foresight of all or any of these.—4. That both elect and non-elect, are considered alike, and are upon an equal footing in the decree of Predestination; as those that are for the corrupt mass, they suppose that they were both considered in it equally alike; so that there was nothing in the one, that was not in the other, which was a reason why the one should be chosen, and the other lfft: so those that are for the pure mass, suppose both to be considered in the same, and as not yet born, and having done neither good nor evil.—5. That it is an eternal

the spirit and belief of the truth" (2 Thes 2:13). "A new heart also will I give you, and a new spirit will I put within you: and I will take away the stony heart out of your flesh, and I will give you a heart of flesh. And I will put My spirit within you, and cause you to walk in My statutes, and ye shall keep My judgments, and do them...Then shall ye remember your own evil ways, and your doings that were not good, and shall loathe yourselves in your own sight for your iniquities and for your abominations" (Eze 36:25-31). Those in whom the Lord hath put His spirit, let them live as they list, and I am very sure they will live godly lives.

3. The Arminian eternal prescience infers as absolute a certainty, and necessity of events, as our predestination doth; for things must be foreordained to be before they can be foreseen that they shall be. Men may argue thus from their ground, "If I be eternally foreseen to believe, I shall believe and be saved." And yet on the contrary they teach men to say, "I can repent when I will; I may be elected whenever I please, though I at present am living in lewdness, for I have a free-will to repent even on my deathbed, so I may be saved if I think proper." This is the doctrine that will make men remiss in duty! But, for an elect soul, by the operation of the Holy Spirit, to read the heart of his covenant God towards him as loving him everlastingly, absolutely, and peculiarly; and, in consequence of His everlasting unchangeable love, bestowing on him, and giving for him, His

---

act in God, and not temporal; or which commenced not in time, but from all eternity; for it is not the opinion of the sublapsarians, that God passed the decree of election after men were actually created and fallen; only that they were considered in the divine mind, from all eternity, in the decree of election, as if they were created and fallen; wherefore, though they differ in the consideration of the object of election, as thus and thus diversified, yet they agree in the thing, and agree to differ, as they should, and not charge one another with unsoundness and heterodoxy; for which there is no reason. Calvin was for the corrupt mass; Beza, who was co-pastor with him in the church at Geneva, and his successor, was for the pure mass; and yet they lived in great peace, love, and harmony. The Contra-remonstrants in

greatest, His best gift, even Jesus Christ; let him live as he listeth, this will be his language, aye and his practice also, "For to me to live is Christ, and to die is gain." I love Thee, because Thou hast first loved me; I am constrained thereto by the all-powerful influences of Thy grace; this fleeting world can now afford nothing satisfactory to me. I shall never be satisfied till I am absent from the body and present with the Lord, till I awake with Thy likeness (Php 1:21; 1 Jn 4:19; 2 Co 5:14,15; Ps 17:15.)

Objection 7

The doctrine of absolute reprobation makes men desperate; "Let me do what I can, if I am to be damned I shall be damned: I am under a fatal necessity."

Answer:

1. This is to suck poison out of a sweet flower; to dash against the Rock of ages; to stumble at the Word, whereunto they were appointed (1Pe 2:8). Why hath God ordered all things by an absolute decree for ever? It is "that men should fear before Him" (Eccl 3:14). God acts freely, as the first cause; and man freely, as the second; in concurrence and not by constraint.

2. This objection is well answered in the 17th Article of the Church of England: "For curious and carnal persons taking the spirit of Christ to have continually before their eyes the sentence

---

Holland, when Arminianism first appeared among them, were not agreed in this point; some took one side of the question, and some the other; but they both united against the common adversary, the Arminians.

Dr. Twiss, who was as great a supralapsarian as perhaps ever was, and carried things as high as any man ever did, and as closely studied the point, and as well understood it, and perhaps better than anyone did, and yet he confesses that it was only "apex logicus", a point in logic; and that the difference only lay in the ordering and ranging the decrees of God: and, for my own part, I think both may be taken in; that in the decree of the end, the ultimate end,

of God's predestination, is a most dangerous downfall, by which the devil doth thrust them either into desperation or into wretchedness of most unclean living, no less perilous than desperation."

3. No man may judge himself a reprobate in this life, and so grow desperate; for final disobedience (the only infallible evidence of reprobation) cannot be discovered till death. We are not to question the secret will of God but to pay attention to His revealed will.

4. The Arminian doctrine [God foresaw what *good* courses I would take of *my* own free-will, and so did elect me] is miserable comfort to one whose heart is privy to its myriad departures from God. It was well said by the Psalmist, "Who can understand his errors?" Who can tell how oft he offendeth?" "Cleanse Thou me from secret faults" (Ps 19:12).To tell men (as Arminians do) that they may be justified and sanctified, and God's children, all but glorification; and yet, after this, may become reprobates, and be damned in the end, is desperate doctrine. Truly it is theirs which is the desperate doctrine; whereas our doctrine is only liable to false inferences from carnal persons—from such persons as draw false conclusions from our Lord's words, and said, "Who then can be saved?" (Lk 18:26). Such inferences are not fairly deduced, but corrupt consequences drawn from good premises.

---

the glory of God, for which he does all things, men might be considered in the divine mind as createable, not yet created and fallen; and that in the decree of the means, which, among other things, takes in the mediation of Christ, redemption by him, and the sanctification of the Spirit; they might be considered as created, fallen, and sinful, which these things imply; nor does this suppose separate acts and decrees in God, or any priority and posteriority in them; which in God are but one and together; but our finite minds are obliged to consider them one after another, not being able to take them in together and at once. (From Dr. Gill's Body of Divinity, book 2, chap. 2, on Election.)

"God's ways are just, His counsels wise,
No darkness can prevent His eyes;
No thought can fly, nor thing can move,
Unknown to *Him* that sits above.

He in the thickest darkness dwells,
Performs His work, the cause conceals,
But though His methods are unknown,
Judgment and *Truth* support His throne.

In Heaven, and earth, and air, and seas,
He executes His *firm* decrees;
And by His saints it stands confess'd,
That what *He* does is ever best.

Wait then, my soul, submissive wait,
Prostrate before His awful seat,
And, midst the terrors of His rod,
Trust in a wise and gracious God."

Chapter Two

OF UNIVERSAL REDEMPTION

Universal redemption,—that Christ died for all men, *cannot* be a Gospel truth, because of the following arguments and reasons.

1. *God the Father's election, God the Son's redemption, and God the Holy Ghost's sanctification, must all be of equal extent and latitude*; but universal redemption, in the Arminian sense of it, makes these unequal.

This is clear; for as the Father, Word, and Spirit are One in essence, so are they One in willing, working, and witnessing the redemption of sinners. As there are Three that bear witness on earth, the Spirit, the water, and the blood; so there are Three which bear record in Heaven, the Father, the Word, and the Holy Ghost; "and these Three agree in one" (1 Jn 5:6,8). Whom the Father elects, the Son redeems, and the Holy Ghost sanctifies. If then there be a universal redemption there must be a universal election, and a universal sanctification also, and so, by consequence, a universal salvation. That the Son redeems no more than the Father elects is evident from two scriptures.

The first is Jn 5:23, which declares the Son must be honoured as equal with the Father; but, to say that the Son redeemed all, and the Father elected but few, is to give greater honour to the One than to the Other, and to make an inequality in Their operations. The second scripture is Jn 17:9,10: "All Thine are Mine and all Mine are Thine," etc. They were the Father's by electing love, and they became the Son's by gift and redemption: "Thine they were, and Thou gavest them Me" (Jn 17:6). Christ redeems only those whom the Father gave unto Him. Hence God's "book of life" wherein the number of the elect is recorded, is called also the "Lamb's book of life;" intimating that the number of those elected by the Father is commensurate with those redeemed by the Son. That Christ redeems no greater number than the Spirit sanctifies is evident from 1 Jn 5:6,7; there must be water to sanctify where there is blood to redeem. Christ's oblation is not of larger extent than the Spirit's operation. Thus it is most apparent that all the three Persons in the Trinity have one object and one design of love. They are equal in essence, equal in honour, and equal in operation.

2. The benefits of Christ's death and resurrection are of equal extent in their objects; but the benefit of Christ's resurrection is not extended to all.

That the benefit of Christ's resurrection is not extended to all and everyone alike, but is peculiar to believers, is acknowledged even by the Arminians. That the death and resurrection of Christ are of equal extent in their objects is evident from Rom 8:33,34 (they are both put together), "Who shall lay anything to the charge of God's elect," for whom Christ died? Who can condemn those for whom Christ was raised? Those for whom Christ died and rose again cannot be condemned. "Who was delivered for our offences, and was raised again for our justification" (Rom 4:25). Those that have the fruit of Christ's battle have the fruit of His victory also; but this cannot be said of all men, for on some the wrath of God abideth (Jn 3:36).

3. The benefit of Christ's death and intercession are of equal extent in their objects; but Christ intercedes not for all.

This is expressly declared in Scripture: "I pray not for the world, but for them which Thou hast given Me; for they are Thine" (Jn 17:9). "They are not of the world" (Jn 17:14). Christ's intercession is "not for the world" at large, but only for those whom His Father hath given Him; and reason confirms this, for if Christ interceded for Judas, Pilate, etc., then He would have had a repulse, and was not always heard of the Father; contrary to Jn 11:42. Again, Christ is a High Priest, and the two parts of His priestly office, oblation and presentation, cannot be separated: and they which have a part in the former have part in the latter also. For the presentation doth necessarily imply the oblation, and gives a perpetual force thereto in the sight of God (Heb 9:12). Christ must intercede on the behalf of those whom He hath reconciled to God by His death; and His intercession is a personal presenting of Himself to His Father on behalf of those whom He personated on the Cross. We cannot say that there be some for whom Christ offered Himself upon earth but doth not intercede for in Heaven; this would make Christ but a half-priest to some, and therefore not a faithful High Priest, contrary to sundry scriptures, Isa 53:11,12; 1 Jn 2:1,2; Heb 9:11,12, and Heb 10:19-21.

4. Those for whom Christ died have Christ for their surety; but all have not Christ for a surety.

All are sinners: and every sinner must die, either in himself or his Surety, for "the wages of sin is death." And the suretyship of Christ consists of this, that He died for us (Rom 6:23). He was "made a curse for us," that is, in our stead (Ga 3:13; 2Co 5:21). Judah was surety for Benjamin's safety (Gn 44:32), and Christ is the surety of the new covenant (Heb 7:22); He took upon Him our sins in His death (Isa 53:4-8; 1Pe 2:24). If Christ was a surety for all, then He offered up a satisfaction for all, in becoming sin, and bearing the curse and wrath of God in their stead. But this is not done for all; for Christ knows not workers of iniquity, and of them He says, "I never knew you" (Mt 7:23); yet He knows His sheep, and He laid down His life for them (Jn 10:11-15).

5. *If the covenant of grace be not to all, then Christ died not for all.*

Christ's blood is called "the blood of the covenant" (Heb 9:20), and "the blood of the New Testament" (Mt 26:28). That the covenant of grace is not extended to all is evident, for it is made with the house of Israel only. "This shall be the covenant that I will make with the house of Israel after those days; saith the Lord, I will put My law in their inward parts, and write it in their hearts; and will be their God, and they shall be My people" (Jer 31:33). The covenant is with those only in whose hearts the conditions are effectually wrought, to wit, putting God's fear therein, and writing His law in their minds, which the election only obtains. None dare say that God entered into covenant of grace with the "seed" of the serpent, but only with those whose "heel" the serpent hurts (Gn 3:15).

6. *If Christ died for His sheep, His friends, and His church only, then He died not for all.*

This is plain from several scriptures. "The good Shepherd giveth His life for the sheep... (I) know My sheep, and am known of Mine... and I lay down My life for My sheep" (Jn 10:11-15). "Greater love hath no man than this, that a man lay down his life for his friends. Ye are My friends" (Jn 5:13, 14). "Feed the church, which He hath purchased with His own blood" (Acts 20:28). "Christ loved the church, and gave Himself for it" (Eph 5:25). Christ died for such as were Paul and Titus, not such as were Pharaoh and Judas, who were "goats" and not "sheep" (Mt 25:33). He died to save "His people from their sins," and therefore His name was called Jesus (Mt 1:21); who are called the "redeemed of the Lord" (Ps 107:2). Now since those for whom Christ died are such as "hear His voice and follow Him," to whom He "gives eternal life" (Jn 10:27, 28), such as He sanctifies, and cleanses, and presents to Himself "without spot or wrinkle" (Eph 5:27), and such as He hath "redeemed from all iniquity, to purify them to Himself a peculiar people" (Titus 2:14), such as are His people, His chosen, His children, it cannot be intended for all unless we say that Pharaoh, Judas, etc., were of the sheep, friends, and church of Christ. It is true He died for enemies (Rom 5:10), but it was to reconcile them to God; such were the believing Romans, who being Gentiles, Christ called "other sheep," not of the Jewish fold.

7. *Those for whom Christ's death was intended, to them it must be applied; but it is not applied to all, therefore it was not intended for all.*

The end and design cannot be severed from the action to accomplish that end. Christ's aim being to bestow what he obtains, He obtains nothing but what He applies. He Himself speaks of some from whom the gospel was hid, and of others to whom it was revealed or made known. "Thou hast hid these things from the wise and prudent, and hast revealed them unto babes" (Mt 11:25). The sum total of the intercession of Christ is, that what He has obtained may be applied, (see John 17 throughout).

8. *If Christ died for all, then must all be reconciled to God; but all are not reconciled.*

Sin hinders reconciliation; and Christ's death is a propitiation for sin (Rom 3:25), so that all for whom Christ died must be reconciled to God; the death of Christ is the cause, and reconciliation the effect following the cause. If all be reconciled, all must be saved, and nothing can be laid to the charge of any. Take away the sin, and you acquit the sinner. But to grant such an acquittance and reconciliation to all brings in many absurdities; for upon this hypothesis it follows, 1st that Cain, Pharaoh etc., were reconciled to God by Christ's death when they were (at the time of Christ's dying) in the torments of hell, and never to be delivered therefrom. 2nd, that God damns reconciled persons. 3rd, that God takes double pay for one fault, in punishing both the Surety and the debtor. 4th, that Christ's reconciling of some is ineffectual, etc. But these things are not so; for to those for whom Christ died repentance is granted, and remission of sins (Acts 5:31); to them is given freedom from the slavery of sin, and regeneration to newness of life (Rom 6:6 Heb 2:14,15); on them is bestowed purifying grace, "purifying their hearts by faith" (Acts 15:9); they have the blood of Christ to purge their conscience from dead works, that they may serve the living God (Heb 9:14), and theirs is life eternal: "I give to them eternal life, and they shall never perish" (Jn 10:28). All these fruits are evidences of our reconciliation by Christ's death.

9. *That cannot be a truth which the Scripture nowhere affirms; and it nowhere asserts that Christ died for all men, much less for every man individually; therefore it is not a truth.*

It is true Christ is said to "give His life a ransom for all:" but not for all men, or for every man individually; the Scripture is the best expounder of itself, and the "all" is rendered "many" in Mt 20:28, and Mr 10:45: "The Son of man came to give His life a ransom for many." "My blood is shed for many, for the remission of sins" (Mt 26:28). And it is so frequently restrained to His sheep, friends, church, believers, chosen, and such as are given to Christ, that it must mean some of all sorts; which, in equivalent terms, is clearly expressed in Re 5:9, 10: "Thou hast redeemed us out of every kindred and tongue, and people and nation." Therefore the word "all" must be taken for all the elect, all His church, all His children that the Father hath given Him, etc., not all men universally, and every man individually.

10. *That which opposes the attributes of God ought not to be received; and universal redemption doth so.*

First, It opposes His justice. If Christ redeemed Pharaoh and Judas, then redeemed souls are unjustly damned; this hypothesis sets the death of Christ in direct opposition to God's justice. And how could Christ die for Judas' sin when Christ's death was his very sin?

Second, It opposes His wisdom. As if God should love and hate the same person at the same time; Esau must be loved if Christ is given to die for him, yet hated, as being ordained to death from all eternity.

Third, It opposes His power. If Christ died intentionally (as to God) for all, then God's intentions are frustrated, since all are not saved. Then God is not omnipotent if crossed in His designs by the work of His own hands. And to say that freedom was obtained by Christ's death for those who are not set free is ridiculous, and making a laughing stock of religion.

The Extent of the Atonement

God imposed his wrath due unto, and Christ underwent the pains of hell for, either—

1. All the sins of all men,
2. All the sins of some men, or
3. Some of the sins of all men.

In which case it may be said:

a. That if the last be true, all men have some sins to answer for, and so none are saved.

b. That if the second be true, then Christ, in their stead suffered for all the sins of all the elect in the whole world, and this is the truth.

c. But if the first be the case, why are not all men free from the punishment due unto their sins?

You will say,— Because of unbelief; they will not believe. But this unbelief, is it a sin or is it not? If not, why should they be unpunished for it? If it be, then Christ underwent the punishment due to it or not. If he did, why must that hinder, more than their other for which he died, from partaking of the fruit of his death? If he did not, then he did not die for all their sins. (John Owen)

Objections Against Particular Redemption Answered

Objection 1

What everyone is bound to believe must be true, and it is the duty of all men to believe; therefore Christ must have died for all men.

Answer:

1. Suppose we grant this position, would not the doctrine of discriminating love be thereby destroyed? Would it not be poor

comfort for a distressed soul to believe that Christ died for it, no more than for Judas and all the damned in hell?

2. They to whom the Gospel never came, they who have never heard of the death of Christ, are not bound to believe that Christ died for them. What God reveals is true; but God nowhere reveals that it is His intention that Judas shall believe, or that all shall believe.

3. All have not the Gospel preached to them; and many to whom it is preached only hear the sound of it with the outward ear: they come and go in an attendance thereon as the door upon its hinges, in a way of mere formality. They are not impressed with a sight and sense of their state as sinners. They are not weary and heavy laden because of sin. The proclamation by the gospel trumpet of redemption for sin through Christ's blood is not a joyful sound to them; they know not their need of it. Evangelical repentance is the gift of free grace; faith is the gift of God. What is God's, as a gift to bestow, cannot be man's duty to perform as a condition of salvation. Those who are invited to look to Christ, to come to Him for salvation, are very minutely described: they are the weary and heavy laden with sin, the penitent, the hungry and thirsty soul, etc., etc.; these are the characters invited to come to and believe in Christ, and not all men (Mt 11:28; Isa 55:1; Mr 2:17).

Objection 2

The words "all" and "every," often used in Scripture, must be taken universally.

Answer:

1. "All" and "every" must not be taken for a universal affirmative collectively, and for every man individually, in the common quoted scriptures; but distributively, as in Mt 9:35, where we are told that Christ went about healing every sickness and every disease among the people: that is, any and every kind of disease, for Christ healed not every disease individually. Also in Col 1:28, where "every" is taken distributively three times over, and

must be restricted to those to whom Paul preached.

2. "All" in 1Ti 2:4, cannot be taken for every man individually, since it is not the will of God that all men in this large sense should be saved: for it is His will that some men should be damned, and that very justly, for their sins and transgressions. Unto some men it will be said, "Depart, ye cursed, into everlasting fire." If God willeth all men to be saved, then all men will be saved, for "He (God) doeth according to His will in the army of Heaven, and among the inhabitants of the earth" (Da 4:35). God faileth not, He cannot be disappointed in His own will, for He worketh all things after the counsel thereof.* Again, in Heb 2:9, Jesus is said to "taste death for every [man];" it is in the very next verse restricted to "sons brought to glory," and in Heb 2:11, to "sanctified" ones. 1Ti 2:6 ("who gave Himself a ransom for all") is rendered in the parallel text in Titus 2:14, "who gave Himself for us." Now, who are the persons called "us" in this text? Are they not particularized as "redeemed from all iniquity, purified and made a peculiar people?" For "all" of this description Christ gave Himself a ransom, and for none else.

The prophet David saith, "All men are liars;" take the word strictly, and he must be a liar that saith so.

---

* " I rather think that by all men, in 1 Tim. ii. 4, are meant the Gentiles, who are sometimes called the World, the Whole World, and Every Creature, Rom. xi 12,15; 1 John, ii. 2; Mark, xvi. 15; which is the sense, I apprehend, in which it is used in verse 1, where the apostle exhorts, that supplications, prayers, intercessions, and thanks, be made for all men, for Kings, and for all in authority; which was contrary to a notion that obtained among the Jews (of whom there were many in the primitive churches) that they should not pray for Heathens and heathen magistrates. The apostle enforces this exhortation from the advantage which would accrue to themselves, 'that we may lead a quiet and peaceable life in all godliness and honesty;' besides, says he, 'this is good and acceptable in the sight of God our Saviour, who will have all men (gentiles as well as Jews) to be saved and to come to the knowledge of the truth, and therefore hath sent his ministers to preach

Objection 3

In John 3:16, and in 1 John 2:2, it is declared that God gave Christ for the "world," and for the sins of the "whole world;" which must be taken literally.

Answer:

1. The word "world" is of various significations. A decree went out that "all the world should be taxed" (Lk 2:1), that is, the Roman empire and such countries in subjection thereto. The faith of the church of Rome was "spoken of throughout the whole world" (Rom 1:8), that is, throughout all the churches, and among all the saints in the world. When the Pharisees said to Christ, "Behold, the world is gone after Him" (Jn 12:19), by reference we find that they meant "much people" who went out of Jerusalem to meet Jesus, crying, "Hosanna" (Jn 12:12,13). The Pharisees themselves, who so said, they were not gone after Christ; therefore the whole world was not gone, they themselves not being gone. So Jn 3:16: "God so loved the world" cannot be understood of the world in a strict sense, for so birds, beasts, fishes, and all inanimate things are comprehended, which cannot have everlasting life; nor can it be the world of men, but as God is the Preserver of both man and beast (Ps 31:6). There is God's love to creatures, His love to men, and His love to good men. God's love was the cause of His sending Christ, and the word "whosoever" (in the verse) restrains this love of God to

---

the gospel among them. For there is one God of Jews and Gentiles; who by his gospel, has taken out of the latter a people for his name and glory. Seeing, then, there are some Jewish notions pointed at, in the context, and the whole is adapted to the state and case of the Gentiles, under the gospel dispensation, there is a good deal of reason to conclude that They are designed here: whereby another principle of the Jews is confuted, which is, that the Gentiles should receive no benefit by the Messiah, when he came; and is the true reason of most, if not of all, those universal expressions, relating to the death of Christ, we meet with in scripture."—Dr. John Gill on 1 Tim. ii. 4, in his *Cause of God and Truth*. A great work, rightly entitled, and is surely a death's blow at the root of Arminianism.

some and not to others. It must therefore be properly God's love to good men, the third love; not such as He found good, but such as He made so.

2. There is a world of believers (Re 5:9); and as manna was only for Israel, so Christ, the true manna, the Bread from Heaven, gives life to the world of believers only (Jn 6:33). Christ was believed on in the world of believers only (1Ti 3:16); the reconciled world (2 Cor 5:19): and "all men have not faith" (2 Thes 3:2). There is also the world of unbelievers. "All the world wondered after the beast. And "they worshipped the dragon" (Re 13:3,4). "The whole world lieth in wickedness" (1 Jn 5:19). The believing world is a world in the world ("these are in the world," Jn 17:11); and they are taken and chosen out of the world. They are in the world, and sojourning among the inhabitants of it as strangers and pilgrims only, this not being their rest, their home; their desires being towards a better country (Heb 11:13-16). And that they are taken and chosen out of the world and given to Christ is clear from Jn 15:19: "If ye were of the world, the world would love its own; but because ye are not of the world, but I have chosen you out of the world, therefore, the world hateth you." Also from Jn 17:6,9: "I have manifested Thy Name unto the men which Thou gavest Me out of the world...I pray for them; I pray not for the world."

> "Zion's garden wall'd around,
> Chosen and made peculiar ground;
> A little spot, enclosed by grace,
> Out of the world's wide wilderness."

3. It is granted that God hath a respect for all mankind. "We trust," saith Paul, "in the living God, who is the Saviour," i.e., the Preserver, "of all men, especially of those that believe" (1Ti 4:10). "The Lord is good to all, and His tender mercies are over all His works" (Ps 145:9). "He maketh His sun to rise on the evil and on the good; and sendeth rain on the just and on the unjust" (Mt 5:45). All this implies not eternal preservation, but only temporal providence and preservation; for the wages of sin

would have been paid at the birth of it, and the world (through confusion by sin) would have fallen about Adam's ears, had not Christ been the glorious undertaker.

All that are redeemed are redeemed by Christ; but the elect only are given to Him; they alone have an interest in Him, are redeemed by Him, and they shall be glorified with Him.

4. The word "world" is sometimes in Scripture put for Gentiles in opposition to Jews, and so it is in 1 Jn 2:2. John wrote to the Jews, and ministered unto the circumcision (see Ga 2:9), and he says unto them, "Christ is the propitiation for our sins, and not for ours only, but also for the sins of the whole world," that is, not for the Jews only, but for the Gentiles also. The Jewish nation considered themselves as the peculiar people of God; and so they were, for to them "pertained the adoption, and the glory, and the covenants, and the giving of the law, and the service of God, and the promises." And Christ was a Jew, "of whom concerning the flesh Christ came" (Rom 9:4,5). The Jews were always taught to appropriate the Messiah exclusively to themselves, to the utter rejection of the Gentiles, who were called "strangers," "uncircumcised," "common," "unclean," "dogs," etc. And it was unlawful for a Jew to keep company or have any dealings with a Gentile (see Mt 10:5; Mr 7:17; Acts 10:28, and Acts 11:3). The salvation of the Gentiles is in various parts of Scripture called a "mystery," "hidden mystery;" the "mystery of Christ which in other ages was not made known unto the sons of men ... that the Gentiles should be fellow heirs" (Eph 3:4-6; Col 1:27). But when this mystery was revealed and made fully known by the divine mission to Paul, who was by Christ sent to preach to the Gentiles (Acts 26:17,18), when it was declared by the vision of the unclean beasts and the Lord's consequent commission to Peter (Acts 10:9-15,20), then the contentions of the circumcision ceased (Acts 11:2,3); they found "the middle wall of partition" between Jew and Gentile was "broken down;" the latter, who before were "aliens from the commonwealth of Israel, and strangers to the covenants of promise," being now "brought nigh

by the blood of Christ." They glorified God saying, "Then hath God also to the Gentiles granted repentance unto life." Jesus Christ is not only the propitiation for the sins of us Jews, but for the Gentiles also (Eph 2:11-18).

5. The foregoing is proved from Rom 11:12, where the two words, "world" and "Gentiles," are both used as signifying one and the same thing. "If the fall of them (Jews) be the riches of the world, and the diminishing of them the riches of the Gentiles; how much more their fullness?"

> "It was a controversy agitated among the Jewish doctors whether, when the Messiah came, the Gentiles, the 'world' should have any benefit by Him. The majority was exceeding large on the negative of the question; only some few, as old Simeon and others, knew that He should be 'a light to lighten the Gentiles,' as well as 'the glory of His people of Israel.' The rest concluded that the most severe judgments and dreadful calamities would befall the Gentiles; yea, that they should be cast into hell, in the room of the Israelites"   —Dr. John Gill

Objection 4
Surely Christ hath as much efficacy to save, as Adam to damn, (see Romans 5:17 For if by one man's offence death reigned by one; much more they which receive abundance of grace and of the gift of righteousness shall reign in life by one, Jesus Christ.)

Answer:
1. There is a difference between a necessary extension and a voluntary one. Adam's sin was extensive necessarily, but salvation by Christ is of free grace, wholly of God's pleasure, and is therefore called the "free gift" (Rom 5:15).

2. Christ is nowhere compared to Adam in the extent of His object, but only in the efficacy of His obedience. All, and everyone, are not in Christ radically, as they were in Adam; all are not given to Christ; but "as many (saith Christ) as Thou has given Me." As all the offspring of Adam fell by his sin, so all that are

Christ's are saved by His death; as all that are in Adam die, so all that are in Christ are made alive (1 Cor 15:22).

3. That the apostle might not be misunderstood, and the word "all" in Rom 5:18 taken universally, the term of comprehension is varied in the following verse, and "all" is rendered "many." "By the obedience of one shall many be made righteous."

Objection 5

In Rom 14:15, it is said, "destroy not him for whom Christ died." And in 2 Pt 2:1, persons are described as "denying the Lord that bought them."

Answer:

1. Everlasting destruction cannot be intended by the word destroy in Rom 14:15, and the context shows this; for the apostle, throughout the chapter, is exhorting the believing Romans not to contemn or condemn one another on account of things indifferent; neither to destroy the weak believer's peace of mind by doing anything (which although it be indifferent, and not evil in itself) may yet prove a stumbling-block to him. I "am persuaded," says Paul, "that there is nothing unclean of itself; but to him that esteemeth anything unclean, to him it is unclean. If thy brother be grieved with thy meat, now walkest thou not charitably. Destroy not" (by thy conduct in eating meat esteemed by thy brother unclean) the peace of mind of one of the weaklings of that flock "for which Christ died." Put not a stumbling-block, or an occasion of falling or offence in thy weak brother's way (Rom 14:13-15). "Whether therefore ye eat, or drink, or whatsoever ye do, do all to the glory of God. Give none offense" (1 Cor 10:31,32). To the same purport is 1 Corinthians 8 throughout.

2. The persons spoken of in 2 Pt 2:1, as "denying the Lord that bought them," are described by the apostle thus, "false teachers"—hypocritical professors, tares among the wheat (Mt 13:25,38), in whom was never the root of the matter; not bought

and redeemed by Christ from eternal death, but had merely escaped, or abstained, from the pollutions of the world through a theoretical knowledge of the Lord and Saviour Jesus Christ (2 Pt 2:20). To answer certain purposes, they made an outward profession of the gospel, which obliged them for a space to be outwardly moral; associated with the people of God, insinuated themselves into churches*, privily introduced therein damnable heresies. Many followed their pernicious ways, by reason of whom the way of truth was evil spoken of, and they made merchandise of true believers. They continued thus for a while, and then either their sheep's clothing was stripped off them, or they threw it off themselves, and returned back again into the world. They were all this while "goats" and not "sheep;" ravening wolves, not gentle lambs. And Peter closes the chapter concerning them by saying, "It is happened to them according to the true proverb. The dog is turned to its own vomit again, and the sow that was washed to her wallowing in the mire" (2 Pt 2:1-3,17-22).

3. The apostle (2 Pt 2:1) does not appear to be there speaking concerning the purchase of the Redeemer's blood, the name or title, Lord (Greek, depotes), is nowhere else applied to Christ in the New Testament, but to the Father, as in Lk 2:29; Acts 4:24; 2 Tm 2:22; and especially in Jude 4, where "the only Lord God" is distinguished from "our Lord Jesus Christ." And even though it could be proved to apply to Christ in the above text, it may be explained upon the principle that it is no unusual thing with the inspired writers to speak of things not as they actually are, but according to the profession of the party. Thus, for instance, (Mt 13:12): "Whosoever hath, to him shall be given, and he shall have more abundance; but whosoever hath not, from him shall be taken away even that he hath" that is, "which he seemeth to have," as explained in Lk 8:18. Thus apostates are

---

* "There are many In the church, who notwithstanding are not Of the church, and therefore at length shall be cast out: But the full and perfect cleansing of them is deferred to the last day." Beza.

said to be "twice dead," which would seem to import that they had been spiritually alive, though in fact that was never the case, but merely what they professed to be.

4. So that, if we even grant the premises, it only follows that such as think themselves redeemed, or are thought so by others, may blaspheme and perish; yet this makes not all the world redeemed; this can by no means establish the doctrine of Universal Redemption.

Chapter Three

OF FREE-WILL IN THE FALLEN STATE, AND OF EFFECTUAL VOCATION OR CONVERSION TO GOD

The Arminians not only deny election to be an eternal, peculiar, unconditional, and irreversible act of God; and assert that Christ died equally and indiscriminately for every individual of mankind; for them that perish no less than for them that are saved; but they also aver that saving grace is tendered to the acceptance of every man; which he may or may not receive, just as he pleases.* That the regenerating power of the Holy Spirit in conversion is not invincible but is suspended, or depends for its

---

* "I came forward, in the name of God, to remove the thick darkness with which many have covered the sacred writings; and to shew, that such a salvation as it *becomes God* to give, and such as man needs to receive, is, within THE GRASP OF EVERY HUMAN SOUL"!—Adam Clarke, LL.D.

Alas! poor Adam Clarke! Thou camest forward, and didst attempt that, which thou wast *unable to accomplish*. It was not within *thy* grasp!

efficacy on the will of man. That notwithstanding Christ's death, it was possible (in respect of free-will) that all should perish; that now, by His death for all, true grace is given to all; which they may improve, hold fast, and be saved; or despise, neglect, cast away, and be lost!

The will of man is naturally a self-determining power and principle, but hath since the Fall the strong bias of sin upon it. Freedom is radically and originally in the will, not in the understanding; and it is an essential property of it, that it cannot be compelled by any created external agent, in its own free choice. Now it is no wonder, if many mistakes arise about this great engine of the Almighty, since the soul knows not itself but by reflection; and though we know its qualities and operations, yet we know not its essence.

Man is considered in a fourfold state:

1. The state of creation, therein he had free-will either to good or evil, but was necessitated to neither.

2. The state of degeneration, wherein he is a servant to sin, and necessitated to evil.

3. The state of regeneration, wherein he is freed from the slavery and dominion of sin, and from the love of sin, though not at present, from the inbred corruptions and in being of it.

4. The state of glorification, wherein man is both freely and necessarily good, perfect, and happy. In the first estate, man is free; in the second, a slave; in the third, set free; and in the fourth, having a glorious liberty.

The controversy is concerning the second state, wherein we say, that man is under a necessity of sinning, yet free from coercion; he is free to evil, but not to good; which appears by the following arguments:

1. That there is no free-will to good in the fallen estate, is proved from the Fall itself; if man, in the Fall, lost his free-will to good, then it cannot be found in the fallen estate.

The Fall implies: The loss of that original righteousness and perfection wherein man was created. If the other faculties of the soul became depraved, and were stripped of their primitive luster by the Fall, then must the will also be a sharer in that deprivation. Now the depravity of the will is proved by considering the good it hath lost, and the evil it hath gained, through Adam's sin. The good it has lost is sixfold: power, order, stability, prudence, obedience, liberty. The evil it hath gained is a threefold rebellion:

a. Against the counsel of the mind.
b. Against the controls of conscience.
c. Against the commands of God.

This king of the Isle of Man (the will), when he come first out of God's mint, was a curious silver-piece, and shone most gloriously; but now, being fallen among thieves, is robbed of all, hath ashes for beauty, and is a tyrant upon a dunghill; yea, is free from righteousness, but a very slave to sin (Rom 6:17-20). Before the Fall, the will had liberty both to good or evil, to do or not to do; but since the Fall, the will is evil, only evil, and continually evil (Gn 6:5). The whole heart now is evil extensively, only evil intensively, and continually evil protensively.

2. If conversion be a new creation, then fallen man hath not a free- will to good.

A convert is called a "new creature," or a "new creation" in Ga 6:15, and 2Co 5:17. Creation is a production of something out of nothing; but if there be a free-will to do good in man before conversion, then is there something of its own nature spiritually good in unconverted man towards the work of conversion; so can it not be called a new creature. Sure I am every experienced soul finds the contrary in that work; the whole frame is out of frame in the unconverted state and man is a confused chaos, a vast emptiness, when this creating power comes upon him. Yea, a greater power is required to recreate this little world than at first to create the greater; for in this, though there be no pre-existing good matter, yet is there resisting evil matter. The creation of the great world was the work of God's Word (Ps 33:6); of His fingers (Ps 8:3); or of His hands (Ps 102:25). But to restore (the little world) man, requires God's arm (Lk 1:51); nay, Christ set His sides to it (Lk 22:44); it cost Him tears and agony and blood. New qualities and operations are created in us; the will to will well, and the power to do well, are ascribed to this creating almighty power in the effectual conversion of souls to God. "It is God which worketh in you, both to will and to do of His good pleasure" (Php 2:13).

3. If conversion be a new-begetting, or generation, then fallen man hath no free-will to good.

Generation is the motion to a being, and a proceeding into a being; this presupposes that there is no being before; for we are not, we are nothing before we be begotten; as it holds true in generation, so in regeneration: "Of His own will begat He us" (Jas 1:18).* It is not said that God begat us of our wills (yet this should be said were there in us a free-will to good) but of God's will; and till then we are not (1 Cor 1:28).

Unconverted men are nothing creatures.

a. A natural nothing; for what is the great womb whence all things come but nothing?

b. A moral nothing; we are morally worse than nothing, that

---

* I have somewhere read of a simile used by the late Mr. John Wesley, namely, "That a sinner may cherish or *hatch* grace, though he cannot beget it." If this be fact, if a sinner hath this power, of his own free-will; then was Dr. Young right in his *Centaur not Fabulous*, who, addressing himself to man, says— "Is thy consent necessary to finish what is began? Yes; it is in thee to grant, or deny, the request of the Almighty. Heaven intends, decrees, labours, works miracles, for thy welfare. It presses thee, it importunately presses thee to comply. Consider how thou art courted; and by whom: by Father, Son, and Holy Ghost, thy *fellow-laborers* for thy good. So glad all heaven; assert, rescue, ennoble, and with bliss eternal, CROWN THYSELF. For without thee, in the constituted order of things, heaven is UNABLE to do it. Without thee, thou amazing being, there is IMPOTENCE in heaven. *Heaven's Desires Are At Thy mercy.*"!!!

is miserable; "Man is vanity," or as in Hebrew, Adam is Abel, that is, vanity (Ps 39:5); "and a lie" (Ps 62:9). "The heart of the wicked is little worth" (Prv 10:20); neither for use nor service; as a shadow is not useful for war, nor a statue for prayer, so fallen man is unfit for the service of God, for his best actions are sin. All this shows we are nothing, and have not a free-will to good, till begotten of God.

4. If conversion be a new birth, then fallen man hath not a free-will to good. We cannot have a birth of ourselves; a babe cannot be born of itself; nothing can have its original from itself, for it would then be before and after itself; it would be and would not be, at the same time. Thus are we taught to look up above ourselves for our new birth. "Except a man be born again," or from above (Jn 3:3). We are born, not of the flesh, "but of the Spirit" (Jn 3:6). Our first birth is of the earth, earthy; our second birth is from the Lord, Heavenly; "Born of God" (1 Jn 3:9).

5. If conversion be a quickening of one that is dead in sin, then fallen man hath no free-will to good.

This is proved from Eph 2:1: "You hath He quickened who were dead" etc. He doth not say half dead, as the man was that fell among thieves (Lk 10:30); but wholly dead, as to spiritual life. There is no manner of good in us (Rom 7:18). And "we are not sufficient of ourselves to think" a good thought till Christ quickens us (2 Cor 3:5). "Without Him we can do nothing" (Jn 15:5). From Him is our fruit found (Ho 14:8); both the bud of good desires, the blossom of good purposes, and the fruit of good actions. Aaron's rod (a dry stick without a root) is a fit emblem; it budded, blossomed, and brought forth almonds; this was not done by any inward principle or power of nature, but it was solely and wholly the work of God. So Ezekiel's dry bones were made to live; nothing of that life was from themselves, but all from God. Thus it is in this spiritual life; we can contribute nothing by which to dispose ourselves to will that which is truly good; we cannot so much as call Christ Lord, but by the Spirit

(1 Cor 12:3). If there be no life, but through union with Christ, then till we be engrafted into that blessed and bleeding vine we cannot bring forth fruit unto God. And it is not any natural power or principle in us that can engraft us into Christ,* for faith is the engrafting grace, and that is "the gift of God" (Eph 2:8), the grace by which the just live (Hab 2:4), and by which Christ dwells in our hearts (Eph 3:17). Till then we are dead, and have no free-will to good.

6. If regeneration, or recovery from the state of degeneration, be a resurrection, then fallen man hath no free-will to good.

That regeneration is a resurrection is manifest from the following scriptures: "Verily, verily, I say unto you, the hour is coming, and now is, when the dead shall hear the voice of the Son of God: and they that hear shall live" (Jn 5:25). "When we were dead in sins, (He) hath quickened us together with Christ" and "hath raised us up" etc. (Eph 2:5,6). It requires as much power to raise, quicken, and make alive a sinner dead in trespasses and sins, as to raise Christ from the dead (Eph 1:19,20). To raise up Christ, and to work faith in us, requires "the exceeding greatness of His power" (Eph 1:19). Here are three

---

* These, and similar expressions, militate nothing against the doctrine of eternal secret union to Christ:—God's people were one with Christ from everlasting; and it is because they ARE Sons (not to make them Sons) that the Spirit is sent into their hearts, crying, Abba, Father, Gal 4:6. Before effectual calling, the elect cannot be distinguished from the reprobate, neither by themselves nor others. It is by grace we are saved, but it is through faith being wrought in our hearts that we have a *knowledge* of that salvation, Eph 2:8; therefore faith may be said to "engraft into Christ," i. e. *manifests* our union with him, Rom. ix. 24, 25. Paul could say of himself and others, we were chosen in Christ before the foundation of the world, Eph 1:4, but Paul gave no evidence, either to himself or to others, of belonging to Christ, when he assisted at the stoning of Stephen, Acts 7:58, and when he went to the High Priest for letters to Damascus, Acts 9:1, 2; he was then dead in sins; but soon after, when that light which is above the brightness of the Sun, shone into his heait, he became *alive* unto God, through Jesus Christ his Lord.

gradations: power, greatness of power, and as if that were too little, the apostle adds, "according to the working of His mighty power." The original words imply not only a working, but an effectual force in working; such strength as in the arms of valiant men who can do great exploits. Nay more, it is beyond all this, it implies a power that can do all things, an omnipotent power. Surely, had there been an internal principle in us toward this great work, or any free-will in us to good, Paul would not have used those gradations, nor such emphatical, significant expressions. This work of regeneration would not then have required the effectual, forcible power of the valiant arm of God; even such a power as raised up Christ from the dead, by which He was declared to be the Son of God (Rom 1:4).

7. If moral persuasion be altogether insufficient of itself to recover man from his fallen state, then fallen man hath no free-will to do good.

If moral persuasion could recover man, then faith would be an easy work, and not require such mighty power as has just been proved. Christ did more to the raising of Lazarus than morally persuade him to come out of the grave; when Christ said, "Lazarus, come forth" (Jn 11:43) a mighty power went along with the command, which gave effect thereto. It is not enough to persuade a prisoner to come forth, but his chains must be struck off, and the prison doors must be opened (Acts 12:6,7,10); and man is more than a mere prisoner; he is dead in sin, so must have a quickening grace; which moral persuasion can never accomplish.

8. If Christ be All in all (Col 3:11), in matters of salvation, then man is nothing at all as to that work, and hath not in himself a free-will to good.

First. Christ's work is to bore the ear, which before is stopped like the deaf adder's to the voice of the charmer (Ps 58:4,5). Christ gives the understanding ear; "He openeth also their ear to discipline, and commandeth that they return from iniquity"

(Job 36:10). See Ps 40:6, and Isa 50:4, which passages, although spoken of Christ, hold good concerning His people.

Second. Christ opens not only the ear, but the heart also (Acts 16:14). The Lord opened the heart of Lydia, not she her own heart; which she might have done had she a free-will to good. The key of the heart hangs at Christ's girdle. "He that openeth and no man shutteth; and shutteth, and no man openeth" (Re 3:7). Moral persuasion will never prove effectual to open the heart of man.

Third. Besides Christ there is no Saviour (Isa 43:11; Ho 13:4); but free-will Arminianism makes man a co-saviour with Christ; as if there was a halving of it between the grace of Christ and the will of man, and the latter dividing the spoil with the former; yea, deserving the greater share: for if Christ be only a monitor, and persuade to good, then man's own will is the principal author of its own goodness; and he makes himself to differ from others, and hath something, that he received not at conversion, of which to boast before God. "Who maketh thee to differ from another? and what hast thou that thou didst not receive? now if thou didst receive it, why dost thou glory, as if thou hadst not received it?" (1 Cor 4:7). Persuasion leaves the admonished will to its own indifferency, not changing it at all; so man becomes his own saviour, at least Christ is not the only Saviour; how then is Christ All in all?

9. If fallen man must be drawn to goodness, then hath he no free-will to good.

That moral persuasion will not bring a soul to Christ; that man cannot come himself, but must be drawn, is proved from Jn 6:44: "No man can come to Me, except the Father which hath sent Me draw him." Drawing is a bringing of anything out of its course and channel by an influence from without, and not from an innate power or principle from within. In So 1:4, it is not said lead, but "draw;" in drawing there is less will and more power than in leading; and though God draws us strongly, yet He doth it sweetly. As we are drawn, we have not a free-will to good, else man fell in his understanding only, not in his will; yet are we volunteers (Ps 110:3), a willing people; not that Christ finds us so, but makes us so "in the day of His power," and when He speaks to us with a strong hand (Isa 8:11). We are naturally haters of God, and at enmity with Him (Rom 1:30; 8:7), but the Spirit gives a new power to the soul, and then acts and influences that power to good; so draws a God-hater to love Him. This is more than a bare persuasion to a stone to be warm, for God takes away the "heart of stone," and gives a "heart of flesh" (Eze 36:26). God the Spirit gives the inclination to come, and the very power of coming to Christ; and Christ finds nothing that is good in us (Rom 7:18).

10. If the soul of man be passive in effectual calling, then is there in fallen man no free-will to good.

The spirit of grace is compared to a precious liquor that is infused; and the called and chosen of God are styled vessels of mercy. "I will pour upon the house of David... the spirit of grace" etc. (Zec 12:10); "the vessels of mercy prepared unto glory" (Rom 9:23). Now a vessel is a passive receiver of liquor poured into it. "The love of God is shed abroad in our hearts by the Holy Ghost" (Rom 5:5); that is, poured out and infused into God's vessels of mercy. The atmosphere is passive when it receives light, and Adam's body was passive when God inspired it with life; though it was formed and organized, yet was it lifeless and breathless (Gn 2:7). So the will of man (in respect of this first reception of grace) hath neither concurrence nor cooperation active; the Lord is alone in that work. Apart from the influences of Divine grace, it is a very hell to any to be brought from hell; though it be an hell to us to stay after God hath opened our eyes and changed our hearts. Corrupt nature neither can nor will contribute anything to destroy its own corruptions. In the first work, the will moveth not itself, but is moved by God. The will, as a creature, must obey its Creator; yet as a sinful depraved will, it obeys not willingly till "made willing" (Ps 110:3). Man, and the will of man, while in an unregenerate state, may be compared to the tied-up colt in Mr 11:2 (tied and bound with sin's chain), but when "the Lord hath need of him," and the "day of His power" is come, the sinner must then be loosed and let go.

11. To deny grace, irresistible, special grace in conversion, is abominable; and the doctrine of free-will is a denial of this.

The advocates for free-will say, "If a man improves his naturals, God is bound to give him spirituals." What is this but turning grace into debt? And to say that the reason why one believes and another does not arises from the co-operation of the free-will of him that believeth, is to deny special irresistible grace as peculiar to the elect. All which is contrary to these scriptures: Jn 6:37,45; Rom 8:14; 1 Cor 1:23,24; 1 Jn 4:13, and very many others. God's dispensations towards His people are all of free grace. He quickens whom He will (Jn 5:21). The heart of one sinner is caused to melt as wax before the fire and receive God's seal, while the heart of another remains as immovable as marble, and as the rock that cannot be shaken; this is the work of God's gracious dispensation. "He hath mercy on whom He will have mercy, and whom He will He hardeneth" (Rom 9:18). The Spirit blows where it listeth (Jn 3:8). God may drop in grace, even with the first breathings of life, and regenerate a babe as soon as it be brought forth; as John Baptist, who was filled with the Holy Ghost, even from his mother's womb (Lk 1:15). And others He may cast into the womb of the new birth when in the very act of dropping out of the world, at the eleventh, yea, at the twelfth hour, as the thief on the cross. Oh, who can order the ways of grace, and set bounds to the spirit of God in its breathings on man!

12. Free-will brings with it so many absurdities that it cannot be received.

First. It makes man the cause of his own salvation.

Second. It puts grace into man's power, not man's will under the power of grace.

Third. It robs God of the honour of making one to differ from another, and ascribes it to man.

Fourth. It allows man a liberty of boasting to God, saying, "God, I thank Thee that Thou gavest me power to will (yet Thou gavest that to Judas as well as me), but I thank myself for the act of willingness, since I receive from Thee no more than Judas did."

Fifth. It exempts the creature from the power of God, as if man, spider-like, could spin a thread out of his own bowels whereon to climb to Heaven.

Sixth. It maketh man the cause why God willeth this or that; so God must attend on the will of man, and not be infallible in His decrees, nor working all things according to the counsel of His own will (Eph 1:11 Ps 115:3).

Seventh. Then the apostle James lied in saying "every good gift" is from God (Jas 1:17); and Paul also was mistaken in Rom 9:11. He should have said, "It is of man that willeth and runneth," and not, "Of God that showeth mercy."

Objections in Favour of Free-Will Answered

Objection 1

There is a law written in the hearts of fallen mankind (Rom 2:15).

Answer:

1. This is conscience bearing witness of right and wrong (see the same verse, Rom 2:15). Impotency is in the will.

2. Adam begat a son "in his own image" (Gn 5:3), not only as a man, but a sinner. "That which is born of the flesh is flesh" (Jn 3:6). "Who can bring a clean thing out of an unclean? Not one" (Job 14:4). While we are Christless we are without strength (Rom 5:6).

3. The devils have more light than men, yet are they altogether dead in sin, though they believe and tremble (Jas 2:19), and though they confess Christ (Lk 4:34; Mr 1:24). They sin freely, yet cannot avoid it, but must sin.

Objection 2

Why is man blamed for resisting the Spirit, if there is no free-will (Acts 7:51; Mt 23:37).

Answer:

1. Acts 7:51. They resisted the preaching of the Gospel (the outward means of grace) by persecuting the ministers of it. The word "resist" in that passage of Scripture signifies a rushing against, and falling upon in a rude and hostile manner, and fitly expresses their ill- treatment of Christ and His ministers by falling upon them and putting them to death. That is the resistance here particularly designed; see also Acts 7:52. The inward work of the Spirit cannot be resisted; as the creature can neither hinder nor further his own creation, nor the dead their own resurrection, so neither can fallen man hinder or further his conversion.

2. Mt 23:37. This scripture, so common in the mouths and so frequently found in the writings of Arminians, so readily produced by them on almost every occasion against the doctrines of grace — this scripture, taken in its context, will advantage them nothing. "How often would I have gathered," etc., "but ye would not." This gathering does not design a gathering of Jews to Christ internally, by the Spirit and grace of God; but a gathering of them externally, to hear Him preach, so that they might be brought to an assent unto Him as the Messiah.

This reception of Christ would not have been saving faith, but it would have preserved them from that temporal ruin threatened in the following verse (Mt 23:38). This scripture therefore, as Acts 7:51, only respects a resistance to Christ's outward ministry. Jerusalem, i.e., her rulers, received Him not (Jn 7:48), therefore their house is to be desolated (Mt 23:38); the city is one thing and her children another. Here is temporal destruction threatened for neglecting temporal visitations (Lk 19:44). Nationally considered, Jerusalem would have been preserved in its peace had the people, upon the rational opportunity afforded them for receiving the Messiah, accepted Christ under that character.

Objection 3
Why doth God say, "What could I do more to My vineyard?" (Isa 5:4).

Answer:
1. This is not spoken of grace, that God gives to particular men peculiarly; but of great things done for Israel as a nation (Ps 147:19-20). God dealt not so with other nations. "These words are part of a parable, representing the state and condition of the people of the Jews; and the design of it is to show the ingratitude of the Jews in the midst of many favours bestowed on them, and the patience and long-suffering of God towards them, and to vindicate His justice in their ruin as a nation" (Dr. John Gill).

2. God did enough in making man upright, and if he hath lost his uprightness, he must thank himself, and not blame God, who is not bound to restore it. Grace is the Lord's own; he giveth it to whom He will.

Objection 4
Man is a rational creature; his will cannot be determined by anything from without, it being a self-determining principle.

Answer:
1. Irresistible grace takes not away that natural liberty which the will hath by creation, but the depravity of it only; knocking off its fetters, but not destroying its nature. We never enjoy our will so much as when God's will overrules ours. If man can determine his own will, and destroy the liberty of it, then much more God who is the maker of it.

2. To will is from nature, to will well is from grace; spiritual fruit must spring from a spiritual root.

*"Not all the outward forms on earth,
Nor rites that God hath given,
Not will of man, nor blood, nor birth,
Can raise a soul to heaven.*

*The sovereign will of God alone,
Creates us heirs of grace;
Born in the image of His Son,
A new peculiar race.*

*Thus quicken'd souls awake and rise
From the long sleep of death;
On heavenly things they fix their eyes,
And praise employs their breath."*

Chapter Four

OF FINAL PERSEVERANCE

The fifth and last point of Arminianism implies that saving grace is not an abiding principle, but that those who are loved of God, ransomed by Christ, and born again of the Spirit, may (let God wish and strive ever so much to the contrary) throw all away, and perish eternally at last.

The doctrine of the Perseverance of the Saints will therefore be considered in this last chapter; and the position to be defended is: That true and saving grace cannot be totally and finally lost.

For the better understanding of this I shall enquire:

First, What is saving grace?

Second, What is it to fall totally and finally?

Third, What arguments can be assigned, or reasons given, to evidence that this special saving grace cannot be totally and finally lost?

—First Inquiry—
What is Saving Grace?

Answer.

First, negatively. It is not the grace of nature or natural grace, which is two-fold. a.) In the pure estate. The gift of original knowledge and righteousness which was infused into the soul so soon as it had its being in pure nature. b.) In the fallen estate. The Gentiles do by nature the things contained in the law; their conscience bearing them witness, and their thoughts accusing or excusing them, according as they do well or ill (see Rom 2:14,15).

Neither, second, is it supernatural common grace, which is called supernatural, as not attainable by the power of nature or free-will; and common, because given both to the elect and non-elect. As dexterity in callings, given by the Spirit to Bezaleel and Aholiab: "I have filled him with the Spirit of God, in wisdom, and in understanding, and in knowledge, and in all manner of workmanship" etc. (Ex 31:2-6). Ministerial gifts, of which Judas was a partaker. Delight in hearing the Word, as the stony ground hearer (Mt 13:20); and Herod also, who did many things, and who heard John preach gladly (Mr 6:20). These tastes of Heavenly things are given to servants as well as to sons, and differ from saving grace in its subject, original, efficacy, property, duration, event, and final issue.

1. In its subject. Saving grace being peculiar to the elect only, and is no wider than election itself.

2. In its original. Common grace flows from Christ as a Redeemer, but not as their Redeemer; and from the Spirit of Christ assisting but not as indwelling.

3. In its efficacy. Common grace may qualify for a common profession only, where there is a "form of knowledge" (Rom 2:20), and a "form of godliness" (2 Tm 3:5), which doth neither renew the heart, nor raise it above a common frame, yet may do

much for God (with the stony ground) and suffer much for God (with the thorny ground) and yet not be special grace "which the world cannot receive" (Jn 14:17), and which lives, revives and reigns, so that sin cannot have dominion (Rom 6:14). Gifts are but as dead graces, but graces are living gifts.

4. In its property or nature. Common grace is but the ornament, not the substance of a Christian; gifts, indeed, may beautify grace, but grace only sanctifies gifts, as the gold beautified the temple, but it was the temple that sanctified the gold (Mt 23:17). For the eminency of gifts, and the prevalency of sin, a form of godliness and the power of sin may dwell and consist together.

5. In its duration. We acknowledge common grace may wither away; it is not a gift that God repents not of, as that gift of effectual calling is (Rom 11:29). The greatest flood of spiritual gifts may decay to less than a drop, whereas the least drop of saving grace shall increase to a river. Thus the Spirit (in gifts of prowess and government) departed from Saul (1Sa 16:14), and ministerial gifts (as the right arm and right eye, Zec 11:17) may fail and be withered up.*

6. In its event and final issue. Common grace aggravates condemnation. As a sinking ship, the more it is laden with gold the deeper it sinks; so men, the more they are laden with gifts without grace the deeper they sink into hell. As a harlot may

---

* Alas, alas, that we live in a day, in which it too often appears that a *gifted* ministry, is more eagerly sought after than a GRACIOUS one! And, after all, what are gifts? Have not wicked men *gifts*?" Madam (said Mr. Grimshaw to a Lady, who was admiring a minister for his great talents and gifts), I am glad you have never seen the Devil, for He has greater talents than all the men in the world; and I am fearful, were you to see him, you would fall in love with him, you seem so highly to regard talents and gifts." I fully coincide with good Mr. Newton, that— "the ground of a minister's *popularity* ought not to convey to him any *solid* satisfaction; for even to Simon Magus, all gave heed from the least to the greatest, saying, 'This

have children but no credit or comfort from them, because they are bastards; so bastard graces, such as false hope, faith, love, etc. (if we are not one with Christ, and married to Him) never end in joy. We may bless ourselves with thoughts of embracing beautiful Rachal (as Jacob did) when in the morning of the resurrection it proves but bleary-eyed Leah.

But Thirdly, and now positively, supernatural saving grace is the sanctification of the Spirit, renewing in us the image of God, and guiding and strengthening us to obedience, and in obedience even to the end. It is His almighty effectual working on the hearts of the elect, giving to them a certain continued connection of all spiritual blessings, which manages them onward even to a state of glory. "Whom He did predestinate, them He also called; and whom He called, them He also justified; and whom He justified, them He also glorified" (Rom 8:30). He "hath made us meet to be partakers of the inheritance of the saints in light" (Col 1:12). The effects of it doth accompany salvation, being permanent effects; both on the soul in justification and adoption, and in the soul in calling, sanctification, and perseverance to glorification. This grace differs not from glory in kind, but only in degree; grace is glory militant, as glory is grace triumphant. Therefore it is called "the riches of His grace" (Eph 1:7), and "the riches of His glory" (Rom 9:23). This is that grace which cannot be totally and finally lost. "The water that I shall give him shall be in him a well of water, springing up into everlasting life" (Jn 4:14).

---

man is the great power of God.' Neither can he ground his satisfaction on the exercise of enlarged *talents*, for even Balaam had extraordinary endowments. Nor yet on Success; for many shall say, * Have we not done many wonderful works, and cast out Devils in thy name?' But a minister's satisfaction must be grounded on His Message. T/ten, no scorn, no reproach that may be cast on him, can take away his Rest. 'His witness is in heaven, his record is on high,' Job, xvi. 19. That was a great character given of one of the old Non-conformists, 'He was a man of primitive Piety and Good Works; zealous both for TRUTH and DUTY; and of unwearied diligence in his work.'"

—Second Inquiry—
What is it to fall totally and finally?

Answer:
1. To fall totally is to have grace altogether dead in us, both in the act and in the habit; no life either in branches, bole, or root; no seed remaining in us, neither any root of the matter.
2. Finally to fall is never to rise again, never to recover by repentance; but to die in sin unrepented of and unpardoned.

—Third Inquiry—
What scriptural arguments can be assigned, or reasons given, to evidence that this special saving grace cannot be totally and finally lost?

Answer:
The following are the arguments and reasons assigned why the chosen of God cannot totally and finally fall away from grace.

1. The first argument is taken from God the Father in His electing love. If the love of the Father to His chosen ones is an unchangeable love (Jer 31:3); if with Him is no variableness, neither shadow of turning, (Jas 1:17); if none can pluck out of the Father's hand (Jn 10:29), then His chosen ones cannot totally and finally fall away. Neither the force nor fraud of hell can prevail against the Father's electing love, which runs parallel with eternity. "God is love" (1 Jn 4:8), the everlasting love must needs flow from an everlasting God. He looketh on His, and saith unto them, "Yea, I have loved thee with an everlasting love" and, therefore, as the effect of it, "I have drawn thee with the cords of loving kindness" (Jer 31:3). It is to be declared of and from the Lord unto the Church, that "The Lord thy God in the midst of thee is mighty; He will save, He will rejoice over thee with joy; He will rest in His love, He will joy over thee with singing" (Zep 3:17). Hence Paul, having spoken of some apostates falling away,

comforts the minds of believers, saying, that their standing is firm, because of election, or rather because of electing love (2 Tm 2:19). This he compares to a foundation and a seal, two things of the greatest validity and security. Believers stand as upon a stable rock, and they are placed as upon a mountain of brass, so cannot totally and finally fall; for the Father is not inconstant in his love; He doth not love today and hate tomorrow.

2. The second argument is taken from God the Son in His redeeming love, which is unalterable.

Thereby are all the members of Christ united unto their Head. Neither principalities nor powers shall be able to separate them from the love of God in Christ (Rom 8:38-39). And the gates of hell cannot prevail against His Church (Mt 16:18). If one member may be broken off from Christ, then all may; one having no more privilege than another in respect of their state and standing; so Christ may be supposed, upon this hypothesis, to be a head without a body or members and to have died in vain; both which are grossly absurd. Christ prayed for perseverance for His; that Peter's faith should not fail (Lk 22:32), and that His disciples should be kept from evil (Jn 17:15), yea, and all believers (Jn 17:20), and what Christ prays for, He is always heard therein (Jn 11:41,42). Christ also promises perseverance to His. "All that the Father giveth Me shall come to Me" (Jn 6:37). He will not utterly withdraw His mercy from them under their severest correction (Ps 89:31-33). "Having loved His own which were in the world, He loveth them unto the end" (Jn 13:1), and loses not one of them (Jn 6:39). He is a Saviour to all parts of the body (Eph 5:23). Saints are in Christ's hands (Dt 33:3), and it is as easy to pluck a star out of Heaven as a saint out of Christ's hands (Jn 10:28); they are all, and they shall all be kept by the power of God, through faith, unto eternal salvation. "Sanctified (set apart) by God the Father, preserved in Jesus Christ, and called" (Jude 1:1 1Pe 1:5).

3. The third argument is taken from God the Holy Ghost, in His sanctification love. If the operation of the Spirit on the hearts of believers be a sure and certain operation, then true believers cannot totally and finally fall away.

The truth of this will appear in that the Spirit's operation is compared in Scripture;

1. To an earnest.
2. To a seal.
3. To a witness.

First, To an earnest. "God hath given unto us the earnest of the Spirit" (2 Cor 5:5). It is the earnest penny of our salvation, not the pawn or pledge, which is to be returned again. The earnest is a part of the bargain, and the first fruits of Heaven. Now the earnest would be lost if the bargain of salvation stand not, and he that hath the earnest be not saved; and if such an one be damned, he carries the earnest of the Spirit along with him into hell, which must needs be absurd.

> "But Christ's to the end shall endure,
> As sure as the earnest is given;
> More happy, but not more secure,
> The glorified spirits in Heaven."

Secondly, To a seal. Faith is our seal; assurance of faith is God's seal. He that believeth hath set to his seal that God is true (Jn 3:33). "After that ye believed ye were sealed" (Eph 1:13). They first believed and then were sealed, i.e., fully assured. God honours our sealing to His truth by His sealing with His Spirit; as the earnest makes the bargain, so the seal ratifies and confirms it. And the broad seal of Heaven must needs be more unalterable than that of the Medes and Persians.

Thirdly, To a witness. "He that believeth hath the witness in himself" (1 Jn 5:10). And there can be no exceptions taken to this witness who abides for ever in the elect, and is called the Spirit of truth (Jn 14:17), which "teacheth you all things, and is truth, and is no lie" (1 Jn 2:27); even the eternal Spirit (Heb 9:14), a witness that can neither die nor lie. So that believers, whose bodies are called "the temple of the Holy Ghost" (1 Cor 6:19), may not become a habitation of devils. This would make Satan rejoice and insult over God (as if stronger than He) could he so dispossess Him, as he is dispossessed by Him (Lk 11:21,22).

4. The fourth argument in defense of final perseverance respects spiritual enemies. If no spiritual enemy can prevail against a true believer totally and finally, then a true believer cannot totally and finally fall away.

1st. Satan cannot; for that wicked one cannot touch them with any of his deadly touches (1 Jn 5:18), but God treads him under their feet (Rom 16:20). The seed of the serpent may nibble at the heels of the seed of the woman, but cannot mortally wound the heart; for his armour is taken away (Lk 11:21), and his works are destroyed (Heb 2:14). Christ in them, the hope of glory, is stronger than he that is in the world (1 Jn 4:4).

2nd. The world cannot; for Christ gives them faith to conquer the world (1 Jn 5:4), yea, He Himself has overcome the world for them (Jn 16:33). He makes them to be higher-region men, above all storms (Prv 15:24); they are made kings unto God; they have a royal spirit to live above the frown and flatteries of the world; and the world, even all sublunary things, are beneath them under their feet.

3rd. Their fleshly lusts cannot; which have not dominion over those that are under grace (Rom 6:14). Though all real Shulamites find the presence of the two armies (So 6:13), the flesh lusting against the Spirit, and the Spirit against the flesh (Ga 5:17), so that they cannot be as they would; yet the issue of the contest is not doubtful. A troop may for a time overcome Gad; coming upon him like bees (as David's phrase is, Ps 118:12), yet Gad shall overcome at the last (Gn 49:19). Believers are more than conquerors, even triumphers, over all their spiritual enemies, through Christ who loves them; and no created power can prevail against them (Rom 8:35-39). Then "thanks be unto God, which always causeth us to triumph in Christ" (2 Cor 2:14).

5. Then nature of saintship proves final perseverance; if saintship be a service, subjection, sonship and marriage, then saints cannot fall away totally and finally.

1st. It is a *service.*—The service of God transcends all other services; men take a servant for a year, and an apprentice for seven years, but our Heavenly master for life. We are to serve God in holiness and righteousness all the days of our lives (Lk 1:74,75). A servant of God is like the Jewish servant that was bored through the ear, in token of perpetual servitude (Dt 15:17). Religion is a perpetual obligation.

2nd. It is *subjection.*—It sets up God to be our King, and our allegiance is for life; it cannot be disclaimed (Mt 19:27). Born of God by the grace of God; and, if we be born subjects into the kingdom of this gracious Lord and King, we must die His subjects; there is no alienation.

3rd. It is a *sonship.*—And this goes beyond the two former similitudes; a servant may be at liberty when his time is expired; a subject may change his earthly sovereign by removing out of his native country; yet a son cannot change his father, and he abides in the house for ever (Jn 8:35). Now as God hath begotten us of His own will by the Spirit of regeneration; causing us to come to him with weeping, and leading us with supplications, because he is our Father (Jer 31:9), and because of the relationship subsisting between Him and us He makes known His *Abba* love to our souls (Ga 3:26). Therefore shall we persevere; God is our Father, and we are called the children of God.

4th. It is a *marriage state,*—and that is for life too (Ho 2:19; Isa 54:5; Re 19:7; Rom 7:1-4), and in this state God hates putting away (Mal 2:16).

6. In respect to the saints themselves, If the names of the saints are written in Heaven; if they are kept for Heaven, as Heaven is kept for them; and if they are compared to things that neither fade nor fail, then they cannot totally and finally fall.

1st. Their names are written in Heaven (Php 4:3; Da 12:1). "Rejoice because your names are written in Heaven" (Lk 10:20). To be enrolled in the book of life must needs hold our perseverance, for there is no blotting or blurring of that book; Satan cannot, for it is above his reach; and God will not, for then his work would not be perfect and glorious if it admitted of blottings.

2nd. Saints are kept as in a double garrison, or as with a guard; Heaven for them, and they for Heaven; they are kept by the power of God through faith unto salvation (1Pe 1:4,5). Christ is their Lord, keeper, and if God had intended the loss of one saint, He would not have invested Christ with all power in Heaven and earth to undertake for His children, and to save them to the very uttermost (Mt 11:27; Heb 7:25).

3rd. Saints are compared to a tree that fades not (Ps 1:3); to a cedar in Lebanon (Ps 92:12; Ho 14:5); to Mount Zion that cannot be moved but abideth for ever (Ps 125:1); and to a house built on a rock (Mt 7:24). Though they fall, God raises them up (Ps 37:24; Prv 24:16). The Lord is with them in their old age (Isa 46:4), and is their guide even unto death (Ps 48:14), so that they cannot totally and finally be lost.

7. The final perseverance of the saints may be argued, seventhly, from the unchangeableness of the covenant of grace.

That which stands upon two unchangeable persons, and ratified before an unchangeable witness, must be itself unchangeable, and the covenant of grace is so.

1st. It stands upon two unchangeable bottoms, even the Word and oath of God. When God made promise to Abraham, He swore by Himself, He being "willing more abundantly to show unto the heirs of promise the immutability of His counsel, confirmed it by an oath" that "we might have a strong consolation" (Heb 6:17,18). God's Word is as gold purified, which loses nothing of its weight, though cast a thousand times into the fire. We commonly say that the bare word of an honest man is as good as a bond. How much more the Word of the God of truth that cannot lie? And this Word is confirmed with an oath, when God swears by His holiness that He will not alter the thing that is gone out of His lips.

2nd. It is made between two unchangeable persons (Mal 3:6; Heb 13:8). In this covenant there is a mutual stipulation. The Father, in covenant, gave to Christ a people (Jn 17:6; 9:12,24). The Son confederates to take man's nature upon Him in the fulness of time; and in that nature to obey, magnify, and make honourable the law, and to answer the demands of Justice in our room and stead, by shedding of His own most precious blood (Ps 40:6,7; Heb 10:5-7; Eph 5:26,27). Hence it is called the blood of the everlasting covenant (Heb 13:20).

3rd. It is ratified before an unchangeable witness, even the Holy Ghost. Indeed the Father and the Son, are their own Witnesses (Jn 5:32,36,37), yet the Holy Ghost is the Witness of that covenant, agreement and stipulation which was between them; as Christ hath a greater witness than that of man, so hath the covenant also, even the witness of the eternal Spirit. Thus the covenant is called "everlasting" (Heb 13:20; Isa 54:8,10; Jer 32:40), and "the sure mercies of David" (Isa 55:3). Sure on God's part, who cannot fail in His good will to the elect, and sure also on their part, who shall have no will to depart from God. The latter is equally covenanted for with the former; therefore though the covenant permits a fall, yet it always ensures repentance after the fall, as in David and Peter, etc. The covenant doth absolutely promise the grace of perseverance, and all things that accompany salvation to the elect, even to the end of their lives.

8. If saving grace be of a permanent nature, and not subject to corruption, then the elect cannot fall from it totally and finally.

Saving grace is called a "seed" remaining in those that are born of God (1 Jn 3:9), and "incorruptible seed" (1 Peter 1:23). Grace never differs from itself, though a gracious man doth from himself. Saving grace cannot be lost, though as respects its acts and operations it may not always be in exercise; but degrees and measures of grace (formerly attained to) may be lost. "Thou hast left thy first love" (Rev. ii. 4), not the habit, neither wholly the exercise of love, but only that vigour and heat that once appeared.

9. The Israelites, who were a type of God's spiritual Israel, could not alienate their inheritance in the land of promise, Lev. xxv. 23, 24; 1 Kings xxi. 3; if this was so in the type, then must it hold true also in the anti-type.

A true Christian cannot alienate his inheritance in heaven, for the deeds concerning this inheritance are written and sealed, and part possession is given the believer even in this life, Jer. xxxii. 40. "I will put My fear in their hearts [present gracious possession] that they shall not depart from Me" [perseverance to glorification]. Christ is able to keep the deposit committed unto Him against that day, 2 Tim. i. 12. He is not only our goel, our near Kinsman, who has redeemed our mortgaged inheritance for us; but He is our feoffee in trust also, keeping heaven for us and us for heaven; and He abideth faithful, 2 Tim. ii. 13, both in drawing, that we should come to Him, and in holding, that we should not depart from Him. Even now is He seated at the right hand of the Father, interceding on our behalf, and saying, "Father, I will that they also whom Thou Nast given Me be with Me where I am, that they may behold My glory, which Thou hast given Me" (John xvii. 24).

> "*His powerful blood did once atone,*
> *And now it pleads before the throne.*"

10. If those that fall totally and finally be not (nor ever were) true believers, then it follows that such as are true believers cannot do so.

The truth of this appears from John viii. 31; those only are Christ's disciples which continue in His word; and such as wholly fall away have but the flashings of a temporary faith, which, like a land flood, fills the country with inundations, yet at last comes to nothing. "They went out from us, because they were not of us" (1 John ii. 19). All true believers continue to the end, Heb. iii. 6, 14; those are God's house and partakers of Christ indeed, and those only.

11. The eleventh argument is taken from the subject of prayer.

Whatsoever true believers ask of the Father in the name of Christ, according to His will, shall assuredly be obtained; John xiv. 13, 14; and 1 John v. 14, 15; and they pray for the grace of perseverance. The church is represented as coming up from the wilderness, leaning on her beloved, Sol. Song viii. 5; convinced of her own weakness, she leaneth on the Strength of Israel, Psalm lxxxiv. 5. "Hold Thou me up, and I shall be safe." "My soul cleaveth to the dust, quicken Thou me. I am Thine, save me" — cause me to persevere (Psalm cxix. 25). These are the petitions of the believing soul, who is convinced that his strength is perfect weakness, his wisdom is folly in the abstract, and that he is not safe from falling one moment, but as supported by the arm of Omnipotence. Believers pray for perseverance, and it is said that they never seek the Lord in vain, Isa. xlv. 19.

12. The last argument for the final perseverance of the saints is taken from the whole concurrent voice of scripture testimony. "The word of the Lord shall stand for ever" (Isa. xl. 8).

Dr. Moulin and others have computed the texts of scripture, which declare the doctrine of the saints' final perseverance at six hundred; the twelve following may, however, suffice (merely as a sample) to establish it as a gospel truth, Rom. xi. 29; John x. 28,

29; Luke xxii. 82; Rom. viii. 30, 38, 40; 1 John ii. 19, 27; 2 Cor. i. 21, 22; Phil. i. 6; 2 Tim. ii. 19; Mal. iii. 6; John xiv. 19; Jer. xxxii. 40; 1 Peter i. 8, 4, 5.

"The Mount Zion of the Lord (Psalm cxxv.) is immoveable. They cannot be removed from the love of God, in which they are rooted and grounded; nor from out of the covenant of grace; nor out of the hands of Christ, out of whose hands none can pluck them; nor can they be removed off Christ, the foundation on which they are laid, which is a sure and an everlasting foundation; nor out of a state of grace in which they stand; neither out of sanctification, which is connected with life everlasting; nor yet of justification, for those who have passed from death unto life shall never enter into condemnation. These, like Mount Zion, abide for ever. They abide on the heart of God, and in the hands of Christ; they abide in the house of God, and among the family of His people. The Lord surrounds them with His love, encompasses them with His favours, guards them by His special providence, watches over them night and day, and keeps them by His power (as in a garrison) through faith unto salvation." — Dr. John Gill

Now if all these things are true, as they most certainly are, *then shall the whole Church finally persevere in grace, and be eternally saved.*

"How oft have sin and Satan strove
To rend my soul from Thee, my God,
But everlasting is Thy love,
And Jesus seals it with His blood.
                    Hallelujah.

The gospel bears my spirit up;
A faithful and unchanging God
Lays the foundation of my hope,
In oaths, and promises, and blood.
                    Hallelujah."

Objections against the Doctrine of Final Perseverance Answered

Objection 1

To teach that grace cannot be lost begets looseness in professors.

Answer:

1. Ah, this is but the state cry of old carnality against the doctrines of grace, viz., that they lead to licentiousness. Swine may trample pearls under their feet, Matt. vii. 6. Ungodly men may and do turn the grace of our God into lasciviousness, Jude 4. Head-knowledge of gospel truths and holy doctrines (the man being destitute of heart experience, and a stranger to the Spirit's work) will never bring forth fruit unto God. It is in the nature of fallen man to love sin. "He drinketh iniquity like water" (Job xv. 16); and it is the work of the Spirit to convince of sin, even of its exceeding sinfulness; without this conviction, no hatred of sin, no love of holiness, whatever the outward profession may be. Satan is glad to see carnal persons professing religion; they are sure (sooner or later) to disgrace that profession, and then the doctrines of grace are charged with being the cause thereof; whereas they have a direct contrary tendency, even "teaching us that, denying ungodliness and worldly lusts, we should live soberly, righteously, and godly in this present world" (Titus ii. 12). The two seeds are minutely described by their fruits in 1 John 3:8-10.

2. Grace may be considered in the being, or well-being thereof. It is, first, radical and fundamental, tending to the being of a saint, as faith, hope, and love; and second, flowing from these for his well-being only, as joy of faith, confidence of hope, zeal and fervency of love; these are the lustre and radiancy of the radical principle; the beams of the sun, as those the sap and substance. The latter we may lose, and perhaps irrecoverably, Psalm 51:12; not so the former. The root remains, though reins be consumed, Job 19:27, 28; it is "a well of water springing up to everlasting life" (John 4:14 and 7:38).

3. There is a divine purpose to be holy even to the end. This is a law written in every renewed will. There is also a divine performance or prosecution of this purpose. This is not always found alike active in a gracious heart. This ebbs and flows according to the Spirit's influence upon us. "How to perform that which is good I find not" (Rom. vii. 18). Our life is not hid in ourselves, but it is hid with Christ in God, Col. 3:3, and this requires our daily dependence on His Spirit, Phil. 2:13, and 4:13. In the practical part, a partial decay may befall our judgments, as in the bewitched Galatians, Gal. 3:1, and our affections may cool, as in the Ephesian Church, Rev. ii. 4. Christ's spouse may be in a drowsy frame, yet her heart awakes, Sol. Song 5:2. Grace may, at times, seem to be lost to a child of God when it is indeed not so. The sun may be eclipsed, yet regain his former lustre; the tree may lose all its fruit and loaves in winter, yet have fresh buddings at spring; Israel flies once, yea twice before her enemies, yet conquer they the land of promise. A troop overcomes Gad, yet Gad overcomes at last. And wherefore all this? "Because I live, ye shall live also" (John xiv. 19).

4. Although all the sins of God's people were imputed to Christ, "The Lord hath laid on Him the iniquity of us all" (Isaiah liii. 6); and although the blood of Christ has cleansed, and an application thereof by the Spirit continues to cleanse from all sin; John i. 29; yet still is sin, what it ever was, exceedingly sinful. And if one sinful thought remains unatoned for by Christ (on behalf of His people), there is evil enough in it to sink to the lowest hell. Though God doth not disinherit us for sin, neither blot us out of the book of life, yet doth He, when we sin against Him, withdraw His favour, and embitter all our comforts. He makes relations (that should be comforts) to become scourges to us, 2 Sam. xii. 11, and fill us with anguish, Psalm xxxviii. 3. Surely many of the children of God have found that the evil they have smarted under for sin, after sin hath been committed, has

been fully commensurate to all the pleasure found in that sin. Could David have foreseen the evil consequences of his sin (in the matter of Uriah's wife), he might have said, "A dear-bought sin thou art like to be to me." Yea, sometimes God may add apprehensions of eternal wrath for sin, without any hope of deliverance, Psa. 87:6, 7. As the covenant Father of His covenant children, their transgressions He visits with the rod, and their iniquity with stripes; nevertheless, His loving-kindness is not removed, neither is His faithfulness suffered to fail, Psa. 89:32, 33. Upon these considerations the doctrine of final perseverance begets no looseness in those who are possessors of the grace of the doctrine, whatever it may in those who are professors only.

Objection 2
It is said of some that they made shipwreck of faith (1Ti 1:19), and a falling from grace may be proved from Heb 6:5, etc.

Answer:
1. It will be granted that to make shipwreck of faith, so as to blaspheme the doctrines of the Gospel which persons once professed, is to fall from the profession of the faith; but then, to fall from doctrine of the Gospel and a profession of it, and to fall from the grace and favour of God, or from the grace of faith, are very different things indeed. The reasons assigned for making shipwreck of faith are shown in 1 Jn 2:19. The stony ground hearers endure "but a while," having no root (Mt 13:21); by and by they are offended, fall away, and are said to give up, or make shipwreck of that which they never possessed but in appearance (Lk 8:18). While some are savingly enlightened by the Spirit of God to see their lost state and condition, their need of salvation by Christ and their interest therein, who shall never perish; there are others who are enlightened only into the scheme of the doctrines of the Gospel; and some of these persons to such a degree as to be able to preach them to others, and yet are themselves entirely destitute of the grace of God. When such fall away, they are no proofs nor instances of the final apostasy of real saints.

2. It is spoken also in Heb 6:5 of such as only taste, but digest not; that have their minds informed, not their hearts reformed; sanctified in profession, not in power. And the apostle was persuaded otherwise of these Hebrews to whom he wrote; he was convinced that their faith was not an historical one, but of the operation of God (Col 2:12), evidenced by their fruits, (Heb 6:9,10; 1Th 1:5).

3. Objections may be multiplied by the impugners of the doctrines of grace, and very conclusive and scriptural replies made thereto; yet, as concerns the final perseverance of true saints, of the Father's beloved sons, the Son's redeemed ones, and the Spirit's sanctified ones, as Christ once dead dies no more, so in His members the life of grace cannot die totally (Rom 6:8,9). Faith is given once to the saints; as we are born but once, so but once again. "This is the Father's will which hath sent Me, that of all which He hath given Me I should lose nothing ... that everyone which seeth the Son, and believeth on Him, may have everlasting life: and I will raise him up at the last day" (John 6:39,40).

> "Not as the world, the Saviour gives:
> He is no fickle friend;
> Whom once He loves, He never leaves,
> But loves him to the end.
>
> Though thousand snares enclose his feet,
> Not one shall hold him fast;
> Whatever dangers he may meet,
> He shall get safe at last.
>
> The spirit that would this truth withstand
> Would pull God's temple down,
> Wrest Jesus' sceptre from His hand,
> And spoil Him of his crown.

Satan might then full victory boast,
The Church might wholly fall;
If one believer may be lost,
It follows, so may all.

But Christ, in every age, has prov'd,
His purchase firm and true;
If this foundation be removed,
What shall the righteous do?"

AN ODE TO SOVEREIGN GRACE
Christopher Ness, 1700

CONCLUSION

And now my dear Christian Reader! in folding up this little Treatise, at the close of the revised thereof for this fourth edition, I bow the knee before my Covenant Father's throne, beseeching Him to bless the perusal to thy soul's benefit.

The old copy was put into my hands (in the year 1810) just about the time when the Lord graciously removed the scales from mine eyes, and gave me to "see out of obscurity and out of darkness." The benefit my soul then received therefrom, is more than by pen or tongue I can describe. And now, after (from that eventful period) more than twenty-five years of mercies and goodness on the Lord's part towards me, and of unworthiness and sins on mine towards him, hath passed over me, I am constrained to acknowledge, to His praise and glory, that he hath preserved me (amid the defections of many, who began well) fixed, and, if possible, more and more established in the great and glorious truths and doctrines advocated and scripturally maintained in the pages of this invaluable book.

As I have now afresh scrupulously examined every sentence, yea, and the wording of every sentence in this Treatise; so the preparing of this new edition has afforded me the sacred employ of, as it were, systematically, and I can say, spiritually, of going over, step by step, those great doctrines of our most holy faith such as—eternal and personal election—divine predestination—particular redemption—effectual calling—and final perseverance to eternal glory, of all the Lord's everlastingly beloved ones in Christ. I hate sought after scripture proof for all those foundation-principles of the gospel; nor have I sought in vain. Like the preacher of old, I have counted one by one, br, as the margin hath it, "weighing one thing after another, to find out the reason," Eccles. vii. 27. The Lord be praised that I have found out the reason; and can declare that, the sum of All the amount is as follows:—

1. That Salvation, from first to last, from election to glorification, is *All Of Grace*; flowing only from the sovereign love, will, and good pleasure of Jehovah, Father, Son, and Holy Ghost—and that herein consists the everlasting security of the people of God.

2. That love could not exist without an object, and the object of God's eternal love was Christ.

ABOUT THE AUTHOR

Christopher Ness (1621-1705) was an English Nonconformist preacher and author.

He wrote *A History and Mystery of the Old and New Testaments*, a work to which Matthew Henry is thought to owe much of his most valuable material for his commentary; *A Protestant Antidote Against the Poison of Popery*; *The Crown and Glory of a Christian*; *A Christian's Walk and Work on Earth*; *A Church History from Adam*, and *A Scripture Prophecy to the End of the World*; *A Discovery of the Person and Period of AntiChrist*; and *An Antidote Against Arminianism*, a small work embodying in a brief form the doctrines on election, predestination, etc., as taught by John Owen, Toplady, and others.

Ness was born on December 22, 1621 at North Cave, in the East Riding of Yorkshire, the son of Thomas Ness, a husbandman there. He was educated at a private school at North Cave, under Lazarus Seaman, and entered St. John's College, Cambridge, on May 17, 1638, where he graduated B.A. and M.A. When 23 years old he settled into Yorkshire, where he became a preacher of independent tenets successively at Cliffe, or South Cliffe Chapel in his native parish, in Holderness, and at Beverley, where he taught a school. On Dr. Winter's election as provost of Trinity College, Dublin, in 1651, Ness was chosen as his successor in the living of Cottingham, near Hull, though it does not appear that he ever received Episcopal orders.

In 1656, he became a preacher at Leeds, and in 1660 he was a lecturer under the vicar, Dr. Lake, afterwards Bishop of Chichester; but his Calvinism clashed with the Arminianism of Dr. Lake, and on St. Bartholomew's day in 1662 he was ejected from his lectureship. After this he became a schoolmaster and private preacher at Clayton, Morley, and Hunslet, all in Yorkshire. At Hunslet he took an indulgence as a Congregationalist in 1672, and a new meeting-house was opened by him on June 3, 1672.

He was excommunicated no less than four times, and when in 1674 or 1675 a *writ de excommunicato capiendo* was issued against him, he removed to London, where he preached to a private congregation in Salisbury Court, Fleet Street. In 1684 he had to conceal himself from the officers of the crown, who had a warrant for his arrest on the charge of publishing an elegy on the death of his friend John Partridge, another Nonconformist minister. He died on December 26, 1705, aged exactly 84 years, and was buried at Bunhill Fields Cemetery.

THE MISSION OF GREAT CHRISTIAN BOOKS

The ministry of Great Christian Books was established to glorify The Lord Jesus Christ and to be used by Him to expand and edify the kingdom of God while we occupy and anticipate Christ's glorious return. Great Christian Books will seek to accomplish this mission by publishing Gospel literature which is biblically faithful, relevant, and practically applicable to many of the serious spiritual needs of mankind upon the beginning of this new millennium. To do so we will always seek to boldly incorporate the truths of Scripture, especially those which were largely articulated as a body of theology during the Protestant Reformation of the sixteenth century and ensuing years. We gladly join our voice in the proclamations of— Scripture Alone, Faith Alone, Grace Alone, Christ Alone, and God's Glory Alone!

Our ministry seeks the blessing of our God as we seek His face to both confirm and support our labors for Him. Our prayers for this work can be summarized by two verses from the Book of Psalms:

"...let the beauty of the LORD our God be upon us, And establish the work of our hands for us; Yes, establish the work of our hands." —Psalm 90:17

"Not unto us, O LORD, not unto us, but to your name give glory." —Psalm 115:1

Great Christian Books appreciates the financial support of anyone who shares our burden and vision for publishing literature which combines sound Bible doctrine and practical exhortation in an age when too few so-called "Christian" publications do the same. We thank you in advance for any assistance you can give us in our labors to fulfill this important mission. May God bless you.

For a catalog of other great Christian books including additional titles on Soteriology.

contact us in
any of the following ways:

write us at:
Great Christian Books
160 37th Street
Lindenhurst, NY 11757

call us at:
(631) 956-0998

find us online:
www.greatchristianbooks.com

email us at:
mail@greatchristianbooks.com

www.ingramcontent.com/pod-product-compliance
Lightning Source LLC
Chambersburg PA
CBHW022120040426
42450CB00006B/773